International Association of Legislation (IAL)
Deutsche Gesellschaft für Gesetzgebung (DGG)

edited by
Prof. Dr. Ulrich Karpen

Volume 20

Robert Zbíral (ed.)

The Cradle of Laws

Drafting and Negotiating Bills within the Executives in Central Europe

HART

Nomos

Reviewers:
Jan Malíř, Czech Academy of Sciences, Institute of State and Law
Wim Voermans, Leiden University

Acknowledgement:
Publication of this book was supported by Czech Science Foundation
(project no. 17-03806S, "Exploring Dark Corner of the Legislative Process:
The Process of Preparing Bills by the Executive").

The Deutsche Nationalbibliothek lists this publication in the
Deutsche Nationalbibliografie; detailed bibliographic data
are available on the Internet at http://dnb.d-nb.de

ISBN   978-3-8487-6465-5 (Print)
          978-3-7489-0589-9 (ePDF)

British Library Cataloguing-in-Publication Data
A catalogue record for this book is available from the British Library.

ISBN: HB (Hart)   978-1-5099-4580-1

Library of Congress Cataloging-in-Publication Data
Zbíral, Robert
The Cradle of Laws
Drafting and Negotiating Bills within the Executives in Central Europe
Robert Zbíral (ed.)
155 pp.
Includes bibliographic references.

ISBN   978-1-5099-4580-1   (hardcover Hart)

Onlineversion
Nomos eLibrary

1st Edition 2020
© Nomos Verlagsgesellschaft, Baden-Baden, Germany 2020. Printed and bound in
Germany.

Contents

Introduction: The role of governments in drafting and negotiating bills

Robert Zbíral

Legislation represents the most important medium through which law is expressed. It is the blood of any modern democratic state, without it, the whole organism would collapse. People elect their representatives based on the promises the politicians made before the elections, and these promises are dominantly turned into outputs through legislation. In this sense, law expressed by legislation is nowadays applied as an instrument to prompt social, institutional or economic change, as a tool aiming to improve the life of the society.[1] There are numerous types of legal acts or even soft law that the public power uses to regulate, but in almost all states statutory laws, that is legal acts adopted by the legislatures (parliaments), remain the by far most important source of law (also called statutes or acts of parliament).

Research of legislation encompasses almost infinite number of issues, which generally revolve around questions of "who legislates?", "how the laws are adopted?" or "what is the content of laws?". Answer to the first question related to legislative process seems to be the easiest: parliaments have been always considered the locus of law-making, it has been in the end the driver behind their establishment and existence. However already decades ago some observers of politics noticed the situation was not so clear-cut and pointed out that it had rather been the government (executive) that affects the outputs of the legislative game much more prominently than parliaments. The supremacy of executives is achieved through two instruments: its agenda setting powers in introducing bills and its (usual) majoritarian control of the parliament. The importance of these powers is expected by almost all theoretical models based on rational choice (neo-

---

1 See W Voermars, 'Legislation and Regulation' in U Karpen and H Xanthaki (eds), *Legislation in Europe: A Comprehensive Guide for Scholars and Practitioners* (Hart 2017) 17-18.

institutionalism) theory.[2] Parliaments may reject or modify bills, but they are not able to propose or pursue alternative policies.[3]

It is thus no wonder that many prominent political science scholars came to the conclusions of executive domination: "…legislators do not legislate. Executive legislates…",[4] "…governments can see to it that laws are passed in the shape which they wish these to have…"[5] or "government is able to impose its will on parliament".[6] Formally the situation was exemplified in 1970s by the formulation of so-called "90 percent rule": about 90 percent of bills are initiated by the executive and about 90 percent of these proposals are adopted by parliaments.[7] The proposition was confirmed empirically at least to some degree by numerous research projects exploring situation in the United States,[8] traditional democracies in Western Europe[9] or states in democratic transition.[10] Data show the figures have remained stable.[11] Obviously the exact values vary based on the features of concrete political system, with parliamentary democracies fitting the rule the best.[12] The superiority of governments in parliamentary

---

2 For a review see K Shepshle, 'Rational Choice Institutionalism' in S Binder et al (eds), *The Oxford Handbook of Political Institutions* (Oxford University Press 2008).

3 See also P Norton, *Parliaments in Western Europe* (Frank Cass 1990) 4-5.

4 R Obler, 'Legislatures and the Survival of Political Systems: A Review Article' (1981) 96 Political Science Quarterly 127.

5 J Blondel, *Comparative Government: An Introduction* (Philip Allan 1990) 241.

6 G Tsebelis, *Veto Players. How Political Institutions Work* (Princeton University Press 2002) 93.

7 The rule was probably first formulated in J Schwarz and E Shaw, *The United States Congress in Comparative Perspective* (Dryden Press 1976) 199; see also D Olson, *The legislative process: A comparative approach* (Harper and Row 1980) 174.

8 G Cox and M McCubbins, *Setting the Agenda. Responsible Party Government in the U.S. House of Representatives* (Cambridge University Press 2005).

9 See contributions in BE Rasch and G Tsebelis (eds), *The Role of Governments in Legislative Agenda Setting* (Routledge, 2011).

10 T Power, 'Time and Legislative Development in New Democracies: Is Executive Dominance Always Irreversible?' in R Pelizzo et al (eds), *Trends in Parliamentary Oversight* (World Bank Institute 2004) 47-54.

11 See e.g. D Altman, *Citizenship and Contemporary Direct Democracy* (Cambridge University Press 2018) 103.

12 E.g. SM Saiegh, 'Political Prowess or "Lady Luck"? Evaluating Chief Executives' Legislative Success Rates' (2009) 71 The Journal of Politics 1342.

systems is so high that some researchers view it as analogous to the single firm in a natural monopoly.[13]

Ulrich Karpen divided the life of laws into regulatory cycle of four phases: a) drafting and initiating, b) deliberation and adoption, c) implementation and enforcement control, d) amendment.[14] Governments are closely involved in all of them, however if we take the abovementioned theoretical (agenda setting powers of the government and its control of parliament) and empirical (90 percent rule) arguments at face value, the first phase of the regulatory cycle has the utmost influence on content and structure of laws. Simply said, bills that the governments submit to the parliaments are in most cases adopted almost unchanged as laws – this conclusion also answers the question "who legislates?". But by accepting that a new research theme opens up. If the role of governments and their bills in the legislative process is so crucial, we need to take a step further and look closer on how the governments prepare and adopt bills, or, to paraphrase Obler above, how the government legislates.

Unfortunately, the inquiry into current state-of-the-art on the role of government in preparing bills rather unearths a "dark corner" of legislative studies. If one reviews the two recently published "bibles" in the field of legislative studies, the political science oriented *Oxford Handbook of Legislative Studies* touches on the topic (cursorily) in only three chapters out of 33,[15] legal science oriented *Legislation in Europe* grants the topic more attention but treats it primarily as crosscutting issue that reaches only minority of chapters.[16] Situation is not very different in journals, the flagship *Journal of Legislative Studies* also concentrates primarily on various aspects of the workings of parliaments or executive-legislative relations.[17] The territory is of course not completely unchartered, but outputs often face the usual "breadth vs depth dilemma". Either they try to illustrate the role of government in preparing bills in its entirety but then the investiga-

---

13 M Crain et al, 'Monopoly Aspects of Political Parties' (1979) 7 Atlantic Economic Journal 542.

14 U Karpen, 'Introduction' in U Karpen and H Xanthaki (eds), *Legislation in Europe: A Comprehensive Guide for Scholars and Practitioners* (Hart, 2017) 9.

15 S Martin et al (eds). *The Oxford Handbook of Legislative Studies* (Oxford University Press 2014).

16 U Karpen and H Xanthaki (eds), *Legislation in Europe: A Comprehensive Guide for Scholars and Practitioners* (Hart, 2017).

17 For example out of 31 articles published in The Journal of Legislative Studies in 2019, only one (indirectly) deals with the question „how executive legislates?".

tion is limited to one state. Classical examples are publications that in more or less detail describe the national legislative process, including the drafting and initiating phase. Even the best representatives of this genre are often written in local languages, have by definition no comparative ambition and focus mostly on legalistic analysis of formal institutional framework and rules.[18] The second strategy aims to involve more cases (states) but then it is possible to involve only certain aspects of the bills' preparation process, for example in legal science we can mention publications dealing with legislative drafting and technique,[19] very popular topic in public administration research is ex-ante or ex-post evaluation of legislation (Regulatory Impact Assessment).[20] There is one book that escaped the dilemma and covered the role of governments in a number of (West European) states, still it focused primarily on formal agenda-setting powers of governments and their control of parliamentary agenda and procedures, while the process of bill's preparation was neglected.[21]

This edited volume attempts to close at least certain parts of the delimited knowledge-gap. Its aim is to describe and analyse process of preparing bills by governments in selected countries. We decided to apply a traditional approach where each chapter informs one case representing one country. The first part of each case study is primarily descriptive and relies on study of legal texts and case-law (if available), the latter part focuses on "law in action" and preferably introduces some elements of political practice, supported by (descriptive) empirical data and concrete examples. As authors were requested to follow predefined framework, knowledge gained from case studies shall be easier to compare.

There are two objections that may be raised to the chosen approach. Firstly that it is too descriptive (legalistic) and not based on comprehen-

---

18 E.g. M Zander, *The Law-Making Process* (Hart 2015) for the United Kingdom; for Germany see H Schneider, *Gesetzgebung: ein Lehr- und Handbuch* (C.F. Müller 2002) or more specifically HG Maasen, 'Gesetzesinitiativen der Bundesregierung' in W Kluth and S Krings (eds), *Gesetzgebung: Rechtsetzung durch Parlamente und Verwaltungen sowie ihre gerichtliche Kontrolle* (C.F. Müller 2015) 191-227; for the Czech Republic D Bohadlo et al (eds), *Legislativní proces (teorie a praxe)* (Ministerstvo vnitra 2011).

19 E.g. H Xanthaki, *Drafting Legislation: Art and Technology of Rules for Regulation* (Hart 2014).

20 For a review see C Dunlop and C Radaelli (eds), *Handbook of Regulatory Impact Assessment* (Edward Elgar 2016).

21 See Rasch and Tsebelis 2011, *ibid.*

sive empirical data collection, or to put it differently, that the research falls under the legal science umbrella. From practical viewpoint, it must be admitted that the chapters are written mostly by lawyers and lawyers (both scholars and practitioners of law-making) are considered the main target group. Yet the choice was not solely practical, it was also closely linked to the abovementioned state-of-the-art. We may of course apply deductive logic and try to formulate and test hypotheses based on well-established formal theories (e.g. neoinstitutionalist, principal-agent, rational choice), but such research design would be premature and methodologically controversial because due to patchy and haphazard terrain of the current knowledge on the topic in question, such propositions will be close to hunches than firmly grounded paradigms.[22] Instead, we need to inductively systemize what is really relevant to our cases and collect enough information to delineate those research designs. The chapters thus concentrate on gaining deep insight into the process of bills' preparation by governments, including the roles of involved subjects (actors) and rules.

The second (potential) drawback of the book is its limited substantive scope. The chapters dominantly encompass only the executive phase of preparatory process, i.e. the period between the presentation of the first draft of the bill and a moment when final draft of the bill is agreed upon by the government. Also this decision was intentional. Obviously we acknowledge that the draft of the bill submitted to the parliament may be significantly changed or even not adopted, but as presented above, empirical data show that these cases are rather rare and the topic of executive-legislative relations has already gained enough attention in the literature. We therefore prefer to put emphasis on the under-researched phase, but some chapters include at least a short section reviewing the fate of governmental bills in further stages of the legislative process.

Another methodological dilemma that requires discussion is the selection of cases. While in general the legislative processes have quite similar sequencing and goals across democratic countries, the numerous distinct features of both the legislative processes and political systems as such

---

22 Or, to use more scientific terminology, they will resemble „ordinary knowledge" as opposed to „usable knowledge", see C Lindblom and D Cohen, *Usable Knowledge - Social Science and Social Problem Solving* (Yale University Press 1979).

make comparisons difficult,[23] causing the mentioned preference of one-case (state) inquiries in the legislative studies. We decided not to follow this "easy" path. Such research project may indeed provide very detailed picture of a situation in the chosen country, however as Giovanni Sartori once quipped: "he who knows one country only knows none".[24] On the other hand, ill-conceived or very wide set of cases will cause a threat (to quote Sartori again) of "treating stones and rabbits as equal" and make any comparison schematic and of little use. In the end, the decision was made to include states from Central Europe, namely Austria, the Czech Republic, Germany, Hungary, Poland and Slovakia. Obviously the selection was primarily affected by practical considerations: the editor of the book originates from the region and it was only natural to involve experts from neighbouring states. However the final pool of cases has firm theoretical backing as well. All covered states evince similar important factors that define our topic, notably: 1) Parliamentary democracy: In all countries the governments form the leading force in the executive branch and control the majority in the legislatures, thus meeting the criteria for having key role in the legislative process. Most often the governments have been coalition-based. 2) Position of laws (statutes) in the legal system: All countries in the sample have civil law (continental) legal systems that put emphasis on written law.[25] To be even more precise, they generally follow German legal tradition insisting on a principle that the most important issues in the state must be regulated with statutes (the so-called "reservation of law").[26] By keeping the main parameters fixed, the most-similar cases design is applied and we compare stones with stones. At the same time the cases provide some variation on independent variables that shall make the analysis (and results) diversified.[27] The sample has for example represen-

---

23 See also W Voermans et al (eds), *Legislative Process in Transition* (Leiden University Press 2012).
24 G Sartori, 'Compare Why and How. Comparing, Miscomparing and the Comparative Method.' in M Dogan and A Kazancigil (eds), *Comparing Nations: Concepts, Strategies, Substance* (Blackwell 1994) 16.
25 See A Grodeland and W Miller, *European Legal Cultures in Transition* (Cambridge University Press 2015).
26 E.g. Y Haibo and Q Qianhong, 'Reservation of Law, Legislation and Human Rights Protection' 2 (2014) China Legal Science 92.
27 See J. Seawright and J Gerring, 'Case Selection Techniques in Case Study Research: A Menu of Qualitative and Quantitative Options' 61 (2008) Political Research Quarterly 294.

tatives of different territorial administration (unitary vs federal states), democratic tradition (long-term vs transitional democracies) or role of non-governmental actors (corporativism vs underdeveloped civil society). Moreover, to put the compact set of cases in a wider perspective, special additional chapter was included that compare current trends in drafting and negotiating bills in civil law states with common law jurisdictions.

Based on the current literature on the topic (including the sources cited above) and practical experience with functioning of the bills' preparatory process shared both by the editor of this book and people he interviewed, the authors of all chapters were asked to try to cover and answer at least partly the following research issues (questions) which combine descriptive and analytic (cross-cutting) dimensions.

Descriptive dimension:

- How is the formal framework of the process of drafting and negotiating bills regulated in legal acts (constitutions, laws, governmental decrees), other official documents (manuals, guidelines) or case-law?
- What are the drivers behind the impetus to prepare a concrete bill? Do the governments implement electoral promises coined in the coalition agreement[28] or just react to external impulses and lobby interests? How much are the ministers able to pursue their own "pet projects"?
- Who is responsible for drafting the original version of a bill? The line ministries, special "independent" institutions along the requests from politicians or is the drafting outsourced to external subjects?
- Are the bills consulted prior or during the drafting process? By whom: other public institutions, invited stakeholders or even general public? Are these consultations public and within sufficiently long timeframe? Does the proposing subject have to resolve the comments and what is their impact?
- Is the "quality" of bills subject to review by any independent subjects? Is the impact of the bills evaluated (regulatory impact assessment)? How transparent, genuine and effective are these processes?
- Does the cabinet really negotiate and vote on the bills during its sessions or is everything set and agreed on beforehand?

---

28 See E Naurin et al (eds), *Party Mandates and Democracy: Making, Breaking, and Keeping Election Pledges in Twelve Countries* (University of Michigan Press 2019).

Analytical dimension:

- Relationship between politicians and bureaucrats: The government is obviously a political actor that formally controls the bills' preparatory process. The indispensable role of administrative staff in this process could however hardly be disputed, the question then arises if the latter group is just an agent that implements political decisions or if it follows own agenda even against the interests of its principal. Results from both theoretical and empirical literature, although often only partly related to the issue discussed in this book, are mixed.[29] One group of sources favours politicians,[30] the other gives upper hand to bureaucrats.[31] The question is how these contradicting findings, often acquired from analysis of well-established democracies, apply to more volatile political and administrative environment of post-transformation states.

- Relationship in coalition governments: The formal right to draft and propose bills is always given to the government as a unitary actor. But the coalition governments face the following dilemma: at the one hand, it shall pursue compromises on the agreed common goals in order to be seen as capable cabinet, on the other, parties in coalition still compete against one another for voters and thus have a tendency to pursue their own goals even against their coalition partners. The question stands if the ministers use their information advantage and exploit it to propose bills with objectives incompatible with the other parties, or, vice-versa, what the coalition partners do to limit this threat of ministerial drift.[32] As in case of the previous research issue, the results are often inconclusive and usually tested on mutual control of coalition partners in the

---

29 Many sources rather focus for example of delegated legislation or role of independent executive agencies.

30 See the list of sources discussed in E Page, *Policy Without Politicians: Bureaucratic Influence in Comparative Perspective* (Oxford University Press 2012).

31 Review in J Huber and Ch Shipan, *Deliberate Discretion?: The Institutional Foundations of Bureaucratic Autonomy* (Cambridge University Press 2002).

32 See e.g. contributions in K Strom et al. (eds), *Cabinets and Coalition Bargaining: The Democratic Life Cycle in Western Europe* (Oxford University Press 2008).

parliamentary phase of law-making.[33] Surprisingly the relationships in the coalition during the executive phase are neglected by researchers.[34]

The authors were invited to respect a common outline for all case studies. Brief overview of constitutional and political system of the country is followed by detailed description of formal dimension of legal and institutional framework of the process of preparing and negotiating bills within the executive ("law in the books" approach). Next section shall concentrate on analysis of practical functioning of the preparatory process, basically by reviving the previous part ("law in action" approach). Lastly a special section is foreseen on the fate of governmental bills in the legislatures.

Despite all drawbacks any research in legislative studies faces, we shall not resign on exploring any aspect of law-making, preferably by setting the inquiry in wider context and comparative perspective. Hopefully this edited volume will shed some light into one of these adverbial dark corners of legislative studies and will reveal "how the governments legislate".

---

33 E.g. L Martin and G Vanberg, *Parliaments and Coalitions: The Role of Legislative Institutions in Multiparty Governance* (Oxford University Press 2011); A Andree et al, 'Trust Is Good, Control Is Better: Multiparty Government and Legislative Organization' 69 (2016) Political Research Quarterly 108-120.

34 A helpful exception being R Zubek and H Klüver, 'Legislative pledges and coalition government' 21 (2015) Party Politics 603-614.

Modern trends in drafting and negotiating bills

Constantin Stefanou and Helen Xanthaki

Models for drafting legislation

Legislative drafting is often viewed as a jurisdiction-specific discipline. However, in recent years, phronetic legislative theory has led the way for closer cooperation amongst drafters and policy officers, for further cooperative analyses on aspects of law making, and for the consequent realisation that comparison leads to lessons learnt. With the parallel development of comparative research methodology and its application to legislative studies, we now look at each other to learn how to legislate better, how to legislative more effectively, and of course how to achieve our legislative goals in a cost-efficient manner.

This chapter addresses the diversity on drafting and negotiating bills, identifies the trends in their constituting components, and concludes on the method that best serves efficacy, effectiveness, and cost efficiency. As legislation is a multi-disciplinary phenomenon, its study can only be interdisciplinary. So is this chapter, co-authored under the prism of political legislative studies and legal legislative studies.

The common aim of lawmakers is to achieve effective legislative texts, namely tests that with the synergy of the other actors in the legislative process can produce the desired regulatory results. However, the process for achieving this common goal is not identical. Broadly speaking, civil and common law countries differ in their approaches. However, it would be simplistic to turn this into a civil v common law divide, as there are no "pure" civil or common law systems, at least not in the Europe of the European Union with its decades of integration and cross-fertilisation. As a result, the core of the trend observed in Europe is that each jurisdiction compensates for the disadvantages of their preferred organisation solution in a different manner.

Centralised v decentralised drafting

It is one of the most difficult question in modern approaches to drafting. In addition, it is difficult because in practice both approaches have their pros and cons. Should legislative drafting be centralised within a jurisdiction or should it be decentralised? As a general rule of thumb, legislative drafting is centralised in common law jurisdictions and decentralised in civil law jurisdictions. Starting with the establishment of a central drafting office in 1869, Britain initiated the logic of a single office for the drafting of all primary legislation in an attempt to combat the "mosaic" of legislation, i.e. each piece of legislation written in a different style from the rest. This practice influenced all common law jurisdictions, which usually have a central drafting unit – sometimes attached to chambers of the Attorney General and often referred to as the Parliamentary Counsel's Office. This centralised drafting office ensures homogeneity of legislation as well as exclusivity of the office in the drafting of legislation.

In contrast, civil law jurisdictions have a decentralised approach. Legislation can be drafted at ministerial level, or at cabinet of ministers level or even at head of state level. Moreover, there are often competing drafts from different sources and in some jurisdictions – mercifully very few – individual members of parliament submit their own, usually poorly drafted, drafts on a variety of topics. Thus, it is not uncommon to have more than one drafts on the very same proposal. Those old enough, will recall how in France the refurbishment of the Louvre attracted drafts from the Ministry of Culture, the Prime Minister's Office and the President's Office – the latter surprised many and the explanation was that the Louvre was a very important symbol of French culture and the image of France itself so the President could be involved. Another feature of civil law drafting is the lack of "exclusivity". Therefore, drafts are produced by civil servant drafters or by professional lawyer drafters or sometimes the origin is unknown as the minister will table a draft, which might be the work of an NGO or translated legislation from another jurisdiction. In civil law there is polyphony in legislative drafting with all its advantages and disadvantages.

The similarities and differences of the two approaches have been examined elsewhere and are often used for comparisons. The question to ask here is how do these differences between common law and civil law jurisdictions affect other aspects of the legislative and policy processes? Perhaps more importantly, do they affect the quality of legislation and the speed of legislative production

Table 1: Characteristics of Common Law v Civil Law jurisdictions in legislative drafting

Common Law	Civil Law
Centralization	Multiple sources of drafting (Decentralization)
Exclusivity of first draft	Unknown origin of the first draft
Instructions	Limited or No-Instructions
Solitary drafter	Drafting committee
Long Training	Short Training
Separation of drafting from policy	Linkage of drafting with policy process
Lack of accompanying documents	Many reports/documents attached

Source: C Stefanou, 'Comparative Legislative Drafting: Comparing Across Legal Systems' (2016) 18 European Journal of Law Reform 123-138.

Prioritising Legislation

Let us start with one of the least explored yet very important starting points, that of prioritising legislation. The topic itself is rarely touched by drafting experts[1] exactly because over the years it is understood that every jurisdiction has its own ways of prioritising legislation. Generally speaking, in most jurisdictions there is formally or informally an institution that prioritizes legislation. In some countries it is the cabinet office or secretariat or committee on legislation while other countries do not have a dedicated unit for this task and send their drafts to the drafting office, which then has to prioritize bills itself. Prioritisation is a process carried out in two levels: (a) the government/executive level, which decides that producing legislation in a particular area is desirable; and (b) the drafting office level, which will translate the policy objectives into specific bills. In both

---

1 See for example: R Nzerem, 'Prioritising Legislative Proposals in the Legislative Process' in A Zammit Borda (ed), *Legislative Drafting* (Routledge 2011) 57-68; also see AW Seidman, RB Seidman and N Abeyeskere, *Legislative Drafting for Democratic Social Change: Manual for Drafters* (Kluwer Law 2001) 53-54; O Birungi Kamugundu, 'Prioritizing Legislation in the Policy Process' in H Xanthaki (ed), *Enhancing Legislative Drafting in the Commonwealth* (Routledge 2015) 85-92.

common and civil law jurisdictions prioritisation is an important event in the political calendar, except that in civil law jurisdictions the process tend to be more informal.

The problem with prioritisation is that most civil services are not open about their formal criteria for prioritisation:

- sometimes there are formal criteria, which are confidential (e.g. UK)
- sometimes there are no formal criteria and prioritization is arbitrary (usually a mixture of informed choice and political choices)
- Sometimes prioritization is purely "political" (e.g. the PM's or the president's office will decide and inform the drafting office)

Despite the lack of detailed research, we recognise some broad criteria for prioritization of legislation. In the section below, we detail five criteria. The list is certainly not exhaustive but it is one that has been taught at the Sir William Dale Centre for Legislative Studies for the last 10-years or so.[2]

1. The importance of the social issue that the proposed legislation affects. The following are considered important (not necessarily in this order).
   a) finance bill (budget)
   b) economic contingencies (e.g. development, growth, currency, trade etc)
   c) social contingencies (e.g. redistribution of wealth, social engineering etc)
   d) international obligations
   e) current popular issue(s)
2. The impact of the proposed legislation. Each type of impact answers a particular question:
   a) economic impact (can we afford it?)
   b) social impact (one size fits all?)
   c) political impact (is it compatible with the aims of the government?)
   d) international impact (what will others say?)

---

2 Based on Seidman, Seidman and Abeyeskere 2000, *ibid*, also see a very interesting comparative application in L Worku, 'Prioritizing Draft Proposals - A Comparative Analysis between Ethiopia and Northern Ireland' (*Abyssinialaw*, 15 June 2015), available at https://www.abyssinialaw.com/blog-posts/item/1489-prioritizing-draft-proposals-a-comparative-analysis-between-ethiopia-and-northern-ireland.

3. The 'do-ability' of proposed legislation in terms of finances and resources. There are three issues to prepare for:
   a) unrealistic or unsuitable proposals will damage the credibility of
      the government and perhaps even the credibility of the country
   b) ability to implement is paramount if proposed legislation is to be
      successful
   c) finances and resources should be considered together
4. The "timing" of proposed legislation. There are two aspects to this:
   a. How quickly the government wants the bill?
      i. political priorities
      ii. financial constraints (e.g. use approved funding or lose it)
   b. How quickly can the drafting office complete the bill?
      i. How long will it take to complete the bill?
      ii. How many other bills are being drafted?
5. The ability of the jurisdiction to draft the proposed legislation. Some
   rather difficult questions here about training:
   a) Are the drafters trained?
   b) Practical limitations often play an important role (e.g. size of draft-
      ing office)?
   c) Transposition of some international agreements requires particular
      skills that some drafting offices lack. Are the drafters trained well
      enough?
   d) Are there any private law firms that can help?

What the above five criteria indicate is not merely that prioritization is a
task primarily influenced by government but that it is political in nature
rather than "technical". In fact, because prioritisation of legislation sets the
tone and direction of government, as a political issue it is usually subject
to public interest concerns as they are determined by reason and experience, and as they are balanced against party political priorities.

Quality and harmonisation of legislative expression

Legislative expression is presented as another difference between common
and civil law drafting. It is suggested that in the common law the aim of

the drafter is precision[3] and accuracy.[4] The aim of the drafter is to provide a legislative text which encompasses all details on the topic[5] so that the text could, at least in theory, stand alone in the regulation of the phenomenon that it sets out to address. But statutes and codes are considered evil.[6] In the common law the drafter introduces a remedy in order to create a right, as remedies precede rights.[7]

A civil law drafting team aims to introduce the main legal concepts that are the necessary means for addressing a social phenomenon. The team rests confident that issues of detail or secondary issues will be regulated via secondary forms of law: a general provision of the civil code will require ministerial decisions to complete the regulation on, for example, divorce.[8] As a result, at least seemingly, the main aim of the civil drafting team is simplicity and concision.[9] The objective of the civil drafting team is to strip the primary provision from all details linking it to time as a means of creating a legislative phrase which will be equally applicable in the future when circumstance might change (for example, criminal procedural provisions on admissible evidence in the criminal trial must be equally applicable when technology allows new types of criminal evidence such as videos, DVD etc.).[10] In other words, the aim of the civil

---

3 LP Pigeon, *Rédaction et interprétation des lois* (Gouvernement du Québec 1986) 19; LP Pigeon, *Drafting and Interpreting Legislation* (Carlswell 1988) 7.

4 J Stark, 'Should the Main Goal of Statutory Drafting Be Accuracy or Clarity?' (1994) 15 Statute Law Review 207; O Lando, 'On legislative style and structure' (2006) 4 European Review of Private Law 476; T Millet, 'A comparison of French and British drafting (with particular reference to their respective nationality laws)' (1986) 7 Statute Law Review 153.

5 Lando 2006, *ibid*, p. 476.

6 K Zweigert and H Kötz, *An Introduction to Comparative Law* (Oxford University Press 1998) 265.

7 W Buckland and AD McNair, *Roman Law and Common Law: A Comparison in Outline* (Cambridge University Press 1952) 399.

8 J Stark, 'The Proper Degree of Generality for Statutes' (2004) 25 Statute Law Review 77–84; O Khan-Freund, C Lévy and B Rudden (eds), *A Source-book on French Law* (Clarendon Press 1990) 233; B Dickson, *Introduction to French Law* (Pitman Publishing 1994) 10-11.

9 JA Clarence-Smith, 'Legislative drafting: English and Continental' (1980) 1 Statute Law Review 21; W Tetley, *Marine Cargo Claims* (Les Éditions Yvon Blais 1988) 45-47.

10 C Pestalozza, 'Gesetzgebung im Rechtsstaat' (1981) 39 Neue Juristische Wochenschrift 2084; B Markesinis, H Unberath and A Johnston, *The German Law of Contract, A Comparative Treatise* (Hart Publishing 2006) 119.

drafting team is to introduce primary provisions which will last the test of time.

However, these rather superficial clichés have given way to the realization that the pursuit of legislative quality and the prolonged cross-fertilisation of European jurisdictions under the umbrella of the European Union has led to an approximation of legislative styles. As legislative effectiveness becomes recognized as a synonym of legislative quality, drafters serve it by aiming to produce a legislative text that, with the synergy of the other actors in the legislative process, can achieve the desired regulatory results (namely, regulatory efficacy).

In short, in their pursuit for legislative quality, civil and common law drafters pursue legislative effectiveness, which puts regulatory efficacy to effect in legislative texts. In their array of arrows, drafters have clarity, precision, and unambiguity of legislative communication. Clarity, which encompasses precision and unambiguity, is enhanced by easified language (namely, language that is pitched at the level of the concrete legislative audiences) and gender inclusive language as an expression clearly setting the subjects of legislative provision.

Of course this commonality of values and tools cannot lead to standardised drafting. But the qualifier of diversity is not common versus civil law. The qualifier here relates to national eccentricities in the legislative environment, in the cultural/societal/religious/financial settings within which a legislative text is destined to serve. Effectiveness requires and accentuates legislative eccentricity, as it requires a tailor-made approach to legislative expression and, consequently, to legislative drafting.

Within legislative drafting as a phronetic discipline, where subjective choices based on theoretical awareness and practical empirical know-how constitute the backbone of the drafting task, standardisation is inconceivable. Even if legislative drafters were to agree on rigid rules that disregard national eccentricities, this agreement would be self-destructive, as lack of adaptability and flexibility in drafting choices would render any rigid rule unable to serve the specific jurisdiction with the specific culture, the specific mores, the specific polity, the specific legal system, at the specific time; as a result, the rigid rule would be ineffective, and therefore adverse to, rather than supportive of, quality of legislation.

It is within this context of subjective prioritisation of legal conventions and empirical experiences that one must now evaluate the common v civil law divide. This remains as one of the national eccentricities that drafters and legislators take into account when making drafting choices. The goal pursued is the same: effectiveness. The virtues pursued are the same: clarity, precision, unambiguity. The tools used are the same across the divide: easified and gender inclusive language. What changes between common and civil law legislative drafting is simply the focus applied by the drafter.

Professionalism in drafting

The eternal debate[11] between those mainly older traditionalists[12] who profess that drafting can only be learnt on the job[13] and those innovationists who recommend a combination of formal and on the job training[14] remains lively. In order to take a stance on this continuing discussion one must inevitably turn to the nature of legislative drafting.[15]

The prevailing view, mostly within the common law world, is that drafting is a pure form of art[16] or a quasi craft.[17] It is this approach to the discipline that supported the mentoring style of training for drafters. If drafting is an art or a craft, then creativity and innovation lies at the core of the task. Rules and conventions bear relative value, and the main task of the drafter is to learn the craft from those with more experience. If one believes that drafting is an art, then formal training is not relevant to drafters.

---

11 For the original version of this chapter see H Xanthaki, *Drafting Legislation: Art and Technology of Rules for Regulation* (2014 Hart Publishers), also H Xanthaki, 'EU Legislative quality post-Lisbon: the challenges of Smart Regulation' (2014) 35 Statute Law Review 66.

12 See MM Hoyt 'Education, Training and Retention of Legislative Draftsmen in Canada' (1979) 5 Commonwealth Law Bulletin 273; also see J Ewens 'Legislative Draftsmen: Their Recruitment and Training' (1983) 57 Australian Law Journal 567-570.

13 Which is the prevalent view in the Commonwealth, see D Hull, 'Commonwealth Survey of Terms and Conditions of Service of Legislative Draftsmen' (1984) 10 Commonwealth Law Bulletin 1359.

14 See C Parkhill, 'Best Practices for Developing Drafting Team Expertise - Australia: Publications and Presentations', Canadian Institute for the Administration of Justice Conference (Ottawa, 11-12 September 2008).

15 For an analysis on the science v art debate, see H Xanthaki 'On transferability of legislative solutions: the functionality test' in C Stefanou and H Xanthaki (eds), *Drafting Legislation: A Modern Approach – in Memoriam of Sir William Dale* (Aldershot 2008) 1.

16 See BG Scharffs, 'Law as Craft' (2001) 45 Vanderbilt Law Review 2339.

17 See C Nutting, 'Legislative Drafting: A Review' (1955) 41 American Bar Association Journal 76.

In other words, if experience is the only thing that really matters, then simply time spent by a senior may offer the apprentice the only opportunity to learn on the job. But is drafting really a liberal skill possessed by enlightened legal scholars who take part in drafting committees on behalf of a variety of ministries and agencies drafting legislation?[18]

Or is drafting a science[19] or technique?[20] This is the prevailing approach in most of the civil law world. If drafting is a science, then there are formal rules and conventions whose inherent teleogenesis manages to produce predictable results, provided that the application is correct. If this approach is followed, then there is plenty of scope for formal training. Drafters may learn the rules and conventions of their science, and the correct way in which these are applied in order to produce predictable results.

But drafting is neither pure science nor pure art. To borrow from Aristotle, drafting is phronesis:[21] the praxis of subjective decision making on factual circumstances or the practical wisdom of the subjective classification of factual circumstances to principals and wisdom as episteme.[22] Phronesis supports the selection of solutions made on the basis of informed yet subjective application of principles on set circumstances.[23] To fulfil their drafting tasks, drafters must: one, be aware of the multitude of often clashing rules and conventions; two, identify the most relevant set of circumstances applicable to the problem; and three have the theoretical knowledge and practical experience to promote the rule or convention that best delivers under the mostly unique circumstances of the problem and within the specific jurisdiction in question[24].

The skills required are: both an understanding of the relevant rules, and wisdom through experience in the application of the most appropriate rule.

---

18 See F Ost and M van de Kerchove, *Jalons pour une Theorie Critique du Droit* (Publications des Facultés universitaires Saint-Louis 1987) 52.

19 See contra Editorial Review (1903) 22 Canadian Law Times 437.

20 In opposition see JC Piris 'The legal orders of the European Union and of the Member States: peculiarities and influences in drafting' (2006) 8 European Journal of Law Reform 1.

21 See Aristotle, *Nichomachean Ethics* (D. Ross trans. 1980).

22 See SU von Kirchmann, *Die Werlosigkeit der Jursprudenz als Wissenschaft* (Verlage von Julius Springer 1848).

23 See E Engle, 'Aristotle, Law and Justice: The Tragic Hero' (2008) 35 Northern Kentucky Law Review 4.

24 See V Crabbe, 'Drafting in developing countries: the problems of importing expertise (19920 4 African Journal of International and Comparative Law 645.

These are the main skills that training in drafting must deliver. And they form the core of the reasoning behind the argument that training in drafting must be both academic and practical, both formal and via mentoring. But before we explore this further, let us clarify which are the rules of drafting, and what is the basis of the drafter's subjective choice when selecting the most appropriate one. The dual nature of drafting, and the dual skill required, makes it impossible to consider a drafter trained without formal academic instruction in combination with lengthy practical hands on experience.[25]

And so, the issue is not one of civil versus common law. It is a universal issue of training drafters in both elements of the dual nature of their task. Does this training lead to a professionalization in drafting? Inevitably so. But professionalization does not necessarily require exclusivity. Drafters mist be fully trained, and in that respect they must be professional drafters. However, they may serve both as drafters and as other types of officers. If they have the luxury of time, that is.

Drafting and policy-making

To most civil law policy experts and legislative drafters, the link between policy making and drafting is obvious. In the civil law tradition, very often members of the drafting committee might be appointed to positions which are responsible for the implementation of the legislation they helped draft. This is a sensible and quite reasonable approach to utilizing personal expertise and intimate knowledge of a new law for the benefit of the state. It is also an implicit acceptance of the link between policy making and drafting, a link which in recent years has been strengthened by the practice of attaching a draft piece of a bill at the and of a policy paper – especially policy papers which follow the German tradition of "Research papers" drafted by policy officers at the request of the minister on different policy areas for which the ministry is responsible.

The common law approach is quite different. "In England and its former colonies, most central office drafters subscribed to the myth that they

---

25 Training is a protracted business stretching to six or seven years and more, see for example S Lortie 'Providing Technical Assistance on Law Drafting' (2010) 31 Statute Law Review 17.

never deal with policy".[26] This myth goes back to 1869 and a statement that Henry Thring – the first ever First Parliamentary Counsel – made that his central drafting unit "considers neither policy nor substance, just form". The statement was made in an attempt to appease the ministries which were unhappy to lose the power to draft legislation and it propagated the "myth" that legislative drafters merely cross the "t's" and dot the "i's" without looking at policy. Almost 150 years after Thring's statement the Office of Parliamentary Counsel in London still avoids getting into any policy questions claiming that their work is legal-technical focusing on form!

The reluctance of drafters to discuss policy stems from the fact that in most instances they are civil servants and as such they must be impartial servants of the state. The substantial discussion of legislation touches on the policy side which, more often than not, takes party-political sides making substantial discussion a controversial issue. A good example, in the common law tradition is the recent UK legislation on Brexit. The EU-withdrawal Bill was drafted by the Office of Parliamentary Counsel, under instructions from the Cabinet.[27] But as the Bill was completed before the EU-UK negotiations had ended the Office of Parliamentary Counsel was essentially asked to devise a way of future-proofing the UKs approach to Brexit irrespective of the outcome of the negotiations. Clearly this went above and beyond a "technical" approach to drafting and as the *European Union (Withdrawal) Act 2018*[28] received the Royal Assent on 26 June 2018, some 4-months before the EU-UK agreement was announced clearly issues of substance had to be taken into consideration.[29]

In contrast, the civil law tradition is to mix policy and politics in the drafting committee. From a practical point of view this also means that the civil service is well-aware of the government's priorities which are neither "secret" nor difficult to ascertain. Political priorities and bureaucratic abil-

---

26 Seidman, Seidman and Abeyeskere 2000, *ibid*, p.30.
27 "Legislating for the United Kingdom's withdrawal from the European Union", presented to Parliament by the Secretary of State for Exiting the European Union by Command of Her Majesty, March 2017, Cm 9446.
28 Available at http://www.legislation.gov.uk/ukpga/2018/16/contents/enacted/data.htm.
29 'Draft Agreement on the withdrawal of the United Kingdom of Great Britain and Northern Ireland from the European Union and the European Atomic Energy Community, as agreed at negotiators' level on 14 November 2018', 14 November 2018.

ities are thrown together because the same civil servants present in the drafting committee might be asked to implement policy.

Main legislative actors

It is a basic axiom in modern democracies that decisions are taken by those who have been elected – an axiom which aims to prevent unelected politicians or members of the civil service (including judges) from taking decisions. It is also an axiom of modern western liberal democracies that the state is run by its public administration to ensure continuity and avoid duplication of effort. The two are not mutually exclusive, if anything they work in tandem for the benefit of the state and by extension the people.

So, here comes the difficult question. Is legislation a task for politicians or bureaucrats or both? The obvious answer is that it is the job of politicians but as we analyse and qualify what we mean by legislation the answer becomes more difficult to answer with certainty. Should, for example, we expect individual members of Parliament to table drafts? This is the case in many jurisdictions, but it is clear that such drafts tend to be of low quality. Very few, if any, politicians have had training in drafting legislation and drafting long and complex Bills is not really a task suited to untrained amateurs. Even in the US, where legal aides are used to translating the wishes of parliamentarians into specific bills, it is those members of the Congress or the Senate who employ professional drafters who tend to produce "quality" proposals.

In the common law tradition, producing legislation is a joint task. The government (90% of all bills originate from government) and the civil service join forces to produce legislation, each with their own professional tasks with parliament being the ultimate decision maker. So, the rule of thumb position is that policy belongs to the politicians (certainly initiation of policy), law to the lawyers and decision making to parliament. In contrast, the civil law tradition tends to see legislation as a continuous interaction between politicians and bureaucrats because the roles are not distinct. In many civil law jurisdictions legislation is produced by drafting committees which include bureaucrats, politicians, academics and even judges. Members of the drafting committee have different tasks at different times and it is interesting to note that in recent years in the civil law family the word "technical" is used increasingly to denote (a) the drafting of normative acts in general and legislation in particular, and (b) the competence of ministries to produce subject legislation (what in the common law family we refer to as delegated legislation).

In all jurisdictions the government is the main legislative actor. However, depending on the family of legal system and the idiosyncrasies of individual jurisdictions the other actors emerging are the civil service, political parties and individual parliamentarians. In the last four decades we should also add NGOs (under the broad aegis of "interest groups"), some of whom are now pursuing their policy objectives in parliament and are known to produce drafts of bills, as legislative actors.[30] In the developing world drafts from "donors" are a major source of legislative activity and this is the case in both the common and civil law jurisdictions. Draft legislation originating from interest groups, of course, affects the initiation of legislation – usually regarded as "political" territory. We should note here that the role of interest groups in the so-called fine-tuning of legislation is becoming quite serious and so is NGO involvement in evaluation of legislation.

Of course, external input in the policy and legislative process is always welcome. This is the way proposed bills pass various users' tests and this is certainly the way to expose problems with proposed legislation. The question is "can consultation be beneficial if undertaken on the actual drafting of a bill?" Especially in common law jurisdictions, where drafting tends to be the exclusive task of the civil service, such consultations can be seen as interference. And yet, this practice is increasingly present in common law jurisdictions where drafts of bills are passed by the minister or the attorney general to the central drafting unit and their origin is unknown.

Has this had an adverse effect on the quality of bills, though? It is impossible to give an authoritative answer here for two reasons: Firstly, there is a lack of relevant research in the field. Secondly, and this perhaps explains the lack of relevant research, experts and practitioners have not agreed on a list of specific criteria to be used in order to assess bills. From a practical point of view, this means that it is impossible to assess external involvement in legislative drafting. Instead, each actor offers an impressionistic account of "success" or "failure" based on criteria which can be interpreted in different ways. So, the donor that drafted a bill will claim

---

30 See, for example, how this was received in the early 1980s in WD Costain and AN Costain, 'Interest Groups as Policy Aggregators in the Legislative Process' (1981) 14 Polity 249-272.

some credit for its involvement while, at the same time, the government and its drafting units will undoubtedly claim that all bills are combed by the drafting unit and, therefore, compatibility with governmental priorities is assured. The external researcher trying to assess the process, identify actors and isolate good or bad practices will find it difficult to make any sense unless they have privileged information. This has been the case for many decades and, unfortunately, we only now developing a credible tool for assessment.

Cross-cutting issues

Precious little research has been done in the role of a political system in the development of legislation. The general assumption has been that western liberal democracies tend to face similar problems while the common law and civil law families have their well-known differences in the production of legislation. Mostly these assumptions have been correct in the sense that western liberal democracies do not have systems which affect negatively the law-making capacity. However, over the years we have noticed that certain aspects of the political system may have an effect on the process of creating law. For example, strong governments tend to be more efficient in producing legislation, in this sense electoral systems seem to be important. As the Electoral Knowledge Network points out:

The prospects for a stable and efficient government are not determined by the electoral system alone, but the results a system produces can contribute to stability in a number of important respects.

The key questions are:

* whether voters perceive the system to be fair,
* whether government can efficiently enact legislation and govern, and
* whether the system avoids discriminating against particular parties or interest groups.[31]

Clearly coalition governments and electoral systems which tend to produce coalition governments might be seen as problematic in terms of strong or steady government and for good reason. A government with a clear majority will pursue its objectives in a more direct manner and will

---

31 Available at https://aceproject.org/ace-en/topics/es/onePage.

identify specific areas it wished to legislate on without fear of rejection form the coalition partner. During the years of the Conservative-Liberal coalition in the UK the Office of Parliamentary Counsel had to cater for last minute changes in proposed bills and was prisoner to the day-to-day haggling of coalition politics which made long-term planning for the drafting of bills somewhat difficult. In a system built around the idea of strong government (which simple majority systems tend to produce) such changes can be debilitating. In such systems the opposition plays a minor role, the government legislates without obstacles and private members' bills are either adopted by government or left to their own devises (and usually fail). As far as producing legislation, such systems are conducive to "centralized monophony", i.e. one draft bill produced by a specific actor (the centralized drafting office).

In contrast, in jurisdictions where the electoral system aims to be more representative (usually where proportional representation or mixed systems are used) it is accepted that coalitions will be a more common occurrence, that private members' bills are frequent and may produce legislation, and that the government needs to strike deals to legislate. The role of the opposition is more crucial and from the point of view of producing legislation "decentralized-polyphony" is the norm, i.e. more than one draft bills produced and submitted by different legislative actors.

It is worth pointing out here that there is a certain myth about electoral systems which produce weak governments but strong democracies, as if electoral systems which produce strong governments have an inherent democratic deficit. Democracy can be strong in both. Similarly, producing legislation is neither better or worse depending on the type of government produced – and by extension the electoral system that is in place. Nor is legislation produced by one system or the other more effective. As already pointed out we do not have a generally agreed list of criteria, although we propose some in this chapter.

Conclusions: What is best?

This chapter presented the prevalent trends for negotiating and drafting legislation. The first conclusion arising from this analysis refers to the multitude of options and trends available to jurisdiction in the complex process of taking policy to legislative completion. The second conclusion is that these choices are made on the basis of long-established traditions that interrelate. These cannot be assessed individually, as they are dominos that fall into place in conjunction with the other processes for negotiating and drafting legislation.

Classifications of legal systems are irrelevant here. What matters is not which category each system falls under but how water-tight are the checks and balances that ensure that democracy is served, the legislative process is conducive to efficacy, and the drafting process fertile for effective legislation. At the end of the day, drafting is part of the legislative process, which in turn is part of the policy process. The value of identifying trends is that, through awareness of foreign solutions, it inspires and hopefully instigates self-scrutiny as a means of assessing whether updating current trends via foreign experience could polish away the inevitable deficiencies in negotiating and drafting legislation. It is hoped that this chapter has contributed to awareness, self-scrutiny, and further debate.

Austria

Eric Miklin

Introduction

Like in most modern democracies, also in Austria most legislative propos-als that in the end become adopted are initiated (directly or indirectly) by the government.[1] And again like in most countries, and despite the large number of formal or informal veto-players in the Austrian political sys-tem, bills brought by the government hardly ever fail in parliament (see below). Hence, questions about how government bills are developed and which actors are involved in the process are of crucial importance for un-derstanding legislation in Austria. This even more so, as the amount of parliamentary legislative activities in Austria (that is, the time spent on discussing bills in the plenary or parliamentary committees) is quite low compared to countries like, for example, Germany or the Netherlands – which suggests that in Austria the most important issues usually have been settled already on the pre-parliamentary level.

This chapter shows that, due to political culture that for a long time has been dominated by strong consociationalism[2] and neo-corporatism,[3] pro-cesses of drafting government bills in Austria indeed have been marked by very broad cooperation and coordination between various political actors in the past. However, changes in the 1990's, which can be summarised as a steady move away from a consensus-seeking political system to more

---

1   G Schefbeck, 'Das Parlament' in H Dachs et al (eds), *Politik in Österreich* (Manz Verlag 2006) 152; P Biegelbauer and S Mayer, 'Regulatory impact assessment in Austria: promising regulations, disappointing practices' (2008) 2 Critical Policy Analysis 123.
2   KR Luther and WC Müller, 'Consociationalism and the Austrian political system' (1992) 15 West European Politics 1-15.
3   G Lehmbruch, 'Sozialpartnerschaft in der vergleichenden Politikforschung' in P Gerlich, E Grande and WC Müller (eds), *Sozialpartnerschaft in der Krise* (Böhlau 2003).

majority-based processes of decision-making[4] have significantly affected the process. While coordination between and within ministries is still dense, governments today have become clearly more selective with regard to the external actors they are willing to include. Also their willingness to take into account or incorporate opposing views when drafting their bills has diminished considerably. As a result, government bills today are developed faster, but at the same time less transparent than in the past – helping governments to minimise public scrutiny and hence to shield themselves from potential public critique.

This chapter proceeds as follows: The next section provides a brief introduction into the Austrian political system focusing on those factors that may have an impact on how governments and ministries draft their bills. Section three then introduces the institutional framework, i.e. the official (constitutional) rules, guidelines and recommendations that governments and their ministries are expected to obey. Section four looks into the actual practice of drafting government bills in Austria: To what extent and with what effect do the relevant actors follow the rules and advices provided, and which routines have been established in addition to them? What are the reasons for the process to proceed the way they do? And who is driving the process overall? Finally, section five briefly provides some information on what happens to government bills once they enter parliament and section six concludes.

The Austrian political system and its effect on governments' legislative freedom

The negligible role of the Austrian president

Having a directly elected president, Austria may be classified as a semi-presidential system. The Austrian constitution provides the president with quite some power. Amongst others, he or she appoints, and may dismiss, the government and indirectly (on government proposal) may also dissolve the parliament. For a number of reasons, however, presidents so far have made hardly any use of these rights and their actual role in the politi-

---

4 WC Müller and M Jenny "Business as usual' mit getauschten Rollen oder Konflikt-statt Konsensdemokratie? Parlamentarische Beziehungen unter der ÖVP-FPÖ-Koalition' (2004) 33 Österreichische Zeitschrift für Politikwissenschaft 309-326.

cal process has always been very limited. There is therefore large agreement amongst scholars that, de facto, the Austrian political practice is by and large parliamentarian.[5]

This classification is probably even more accurate when it comes to legislation. Presidents cannot initiate legislation. And while, according to Art. 47 (1-2) of the Austrian Constitution (*Bundes-Verfassunggesetz*, B-VG), all laws in the end require the signature of the president, signature may not be refused based on concerns with regard to the content of the law. Rather, signature simply confirms that the procedure of law-making followed constitutional requirements. So far, no president has ever refused to sign a bill.

Interestingly, an indirect presidential veto-power on legislation could be deduced from the president's constitutional rights to dismiss the government and to dissolve the parliament: To prevent an unwanted law from becoming adopted, the president theoretically could dismiss the government and replace it with one that provides him with a proposal to dissolve parliament before the latter is able to adopt the law. So far, however, no president has ever even adumbrated this option publicly, nor was it used as a bargaining chip in political discussions. Instead, presidential interventions in day-to-day law making so far have been limited to more or less diplomatic comments on publicly contested proposals. Hence, despite the president's constitutional powers, legislative practice in Austria clearly follows a parliamentary logic and there is little need for governments to take the president's views into consideration.

The informal powers of the Austrian Länder

Another mismatch between legal (constitutional) rules and actual legislative practice can be found when looking at another characteristic of the Austrian political system: federalism. Constitutionally, legislative powers of the nine Länder are very limited and there is a strong imbalance between the federal level on the one hand and the regional or local level on the other when it comes to legislation [cf. Art. 10 and 15 (1) B-VG]. In addition, the power of the second chamber of the Austrian parliament, the

---

5 For overview see WC Müller, 'Austria' in E Robert (ed.), *The Politics of Semi-Presidentialism* (1999 Oxford University Press) 22-47.

Federal Council (*Bundesrat*), is very limited. First, it has no power over the federal government. Second, it enters the legislative process only after the first chamber (National Council, *Nationalrat*) has taken its decision. Third, legislative vetoes of the Federal Council in most cases can be easily overruled by the Federal Council with a simple majority (*Beharrungbeschluss*). Actual veto-power is restricted to laws affecting the competences of the nine federal states [Art. 44 (2) B-VG] as well as to constitutional laws concerning the Federal Council itself [Art. 35 (4) B-VG]. So far, the Federal Council has never raised such a veto.

In comparative scholarly literature, Austria therefore has usually been classified as a rather weak form of federalism. According to Lijphart, Austria is a 'centralised federation'.[6] Schultze classifies Austria as 'unitary federal state',[7] while Erk calls it a 'federation without federalism'[8] and Watts sees it as 'one of the most centralised' federal states of all.[9]

A purely constitutional view on Austrian federalism, however, clearly underestimates the actual power of the Austrian states in federal law making.[10] This is, because it neglects the main body through which states de facto seek to influence federal legislation – the State Governors' Conference (*Landeshauptleutekonferenz*). Despite being a completely informal body that lacks any constitutional foundation or legislative powers, there have been numerous occasions in the past, where state governors have been able to prevent national policies from becoming adopted. This 'informal' power of the state governors rests on three pillars. First, they consti-

---

6 A Lijphart, *Patterns of Democracy: Government Forms and Performance in Thirty-six Countries* (Yale University Press 1999).

7 RO Schultze, 'Föderalismus' in D Nohlen (ed), *Lexikon der Politik, Vol. 3: Die westlichen Länder* (1992 Beck Verlag) 108.

8 J Erk, 'Austria: A Federation without Federalism' (2004) 34 Publius - The Journal of Federalism 1.

9 L Watts, *Comparing Federal Systems* (McGill Queen's University Press 1999) 256.

10 For example P Bußjäger, 'Föderalismus durch Macht im Schatten? Österreich und die Landeshauptmännerkonferenz' in *Jahrbuch des Föderalismus 2003. Föderalismus, Subsidiarität und Regionen in Europa* (Nomos 2003) 79-99; F Fallend, 'Austria: From Consensus to Competition and Participation?' in J Loughlin, F Hendriks and A Lidström (eds), *The Oxford Handbook of Local and Regional Democracy in Europe* (Oxford University Press 2010) 173-195; F Karlhofer 'A federation without federalism? Zur Realverfassung der Bund-Länder- Beziehungen' in P Bußjäger (ed), *Kooperativer Föderalismus in Österreich. Beiträge zur Verflechtung von Bund und Ländern* (Braumüller 2009) 131-146.

tutionally combine a number of functions at the same time (head of regional government, head of bureaucracy, main responsibility for 'indirect' federal administration) which makes them the 'outstanding figures of provincial politics'.[11] Second, governors are usually also the leaders (and hence most powerful actors) of their regional parties. Third, the main political parties in Austria are represented both on the regional and the federal level and governors (especially those of the larger states) have a quite powerful position in federal (governing) parties too.

As a result, while constitutionally in most cases there is little need for governments to take regional interests into account, it de facto may be very costly or even impossible to push legislation that runs against regional interests - especially in cases, where the critical regional government and the government on the national level are controlled by the same parties.

Austria's consociationalist and neo-corporatist tradition

Demands for legislative coordination and compromises are strengthened even further through what, at least in the past, may be seen as *the* defining characteristic of Austrian political culture after Second World War: Consociationalism.[12] After strong conflicts between the forerunners of the Social Democratic Party (SPÖ) and the Austrian Peoples Party (ÖVP) in the First Republic, which eventually even resulted in a civil war in 1934, the two parties after the Second World War agreed on a system of mutual acceptance and cooperation as the only fruitful way to proceed. Hence, decision-making in Austria has traditionally been characterised by the ambition to build broad societal compromises and by taking the interests of the 'other' camp into account even at times when only one of the two parties was in government.

The latter was not the case too often anyway, however. Amongst others due to a highly proportional electoral system,[13] (two-party) coalition governments have been the norm for most of the time since 1945 (with single

---

11 Fallend 2010, *ibid*, p. 182.
12 Eg. Luther and Müller 1992, *ibid.*
13 WC Müller, 'Austria: A Complex Electoral System with Subtle Effects' in M Gallagher and P Mitchell (eds), *The Politics of Electoral Systems* (Oxford University Press 2008) 397-416.

party governments in office in only 17 out of 73 years) and grand coalitions have been controlling the government for half the time (36 out of 73 years). Hence, adopting laws in Austria usually requires a compromise between two parties, and for half of the time even compromises between the two largest centre-left and –right parties.

In addition, one of the strongest forms of a neo-corporatist system of decision-making (*Social Partnership*) for a long time assured the involvement of, and compromises between, (amongst others) the large employers- and employees organisations.[14] Throughout the decades, and especially since the late 1990's, however, Austria has moved significantly from a consensus-based to a more majority- and conflict-based political system. Social partners' influence has diminished overall, and their respective impact today depends crucially on whether the party, they have their closest ties with (SPÖ for employees- and ÖVP for employers-organisations) are member of government or not.[15] Also the majorities with which laws are adopted on average have become significantly smaller over time,[16] suggesting that governments today are less willing to take into account the preferences of opposition parties.

The shadow of the Constitutional Court

The last important actor Austrian governments need to consider when drafting their bills is the Constitutional Court (*Verfassungsgerichtshof*), who acts as the guardian of the constitutionality of the laws.[17] While no ex-ante screening of legislative proposals through the Court is foreseen, it may on request review them ex-post and repeal those considered to conflict with constitutional provisions (Art. 137-148 B-VG). As a result, there is a clear anticipative effect in the process of law-making in the sense that decision-makers try to formulate laws in a way that they are likely to pass a potential lawsuit. Linked to this, a Constitutional Service (*Verfassungs-*

---

14 E Tálos and B Kittel, *Gesetzgebung in Österreich. Netzwerke, Akteure und Interaktionen in politischen Entscheidungsprozessen* (WUW 2001).

15 E Tálos, 'Sozialpartnerschaft. Austrokorporatismus am Ende?' in H Dachs et al. (eds), *Politik in Österreich. Das Handbuch* (Manz 2006) 425-442.

16 Müller and Jenny 2004, *ibid.*

17 M Schaden, 'Verfassungsgerichtsbarkeit' in H. Dachs et al. (eds), *Politik in Österreich. Das Handbuch* (Manz 2006).

dienst) until 2017 located at the Federal Chancellery and since then at the Ministry of Justice screens all official government bills ex-ante in view of possible problems.

The Constitutional Court may be by-passed, however, if bills are adopted as constitutional laws. These laws require a two-third majority in the National Council and are considered as being part of the Constitution, which prohibits a review of the Constitutional Court as long as they do not affect one of the Constitution's 'core principles'. Over the years, Austrian governments have time and again used this opportunity to re-enact laws repealed by the Court like, for example, several laws stipulating different retiring ages for women and men (60 and 65 years respectively) initially abolished by the Court in 1990 due to its incompatibility with the principle of equality.[18] The extent, to which the Constitutional Court may restrict a government's room for manoeuvre therefore also depends on the number of seats the latter holds in parliament – and hence whether or not the support of opposition parties is needed to adopt constitutional laws.

The legal framework for preparing governmental bills

According to Art. 41 (1) B-VG, motions brought by the government are one out of five ways to initiate legislation (the others being motions brought by at least five members of the National Council, by one of its committees, by one third of the parliament's Federal Council, or by a public petition supported by at least one percent of the national electorate). For a government bill to enter parliament three formal steps are required: The writing of a ministerial draft, a phase of comprehensive public consultations, and a successful vote on the bill by the government in the Council of Ministers (*Ministerrat*).

For a ministerial draft to be written, an official mandate by the respective minister is needed. Drafts then are developed and written by usually a rather small team of civil servants specialised on the topic at stake. There

---

18 Constitutional Court rulings no. G223/88, G235/88, G33/90, G63/90, G144/90, 6 December 1990.

are a number of official manuals[19] and circulars[20] that provide civil servants with (most of the time advisory) general guidelines regarding the language, techniques of formulation and the formal structure of legal texts. They also provide certain guidelines about the information that should be attached to all legislative drafts like explanatory memoranda. Additional manuals cover, amongst others, topics like how to ensure public participation in the process from the early stages on.[21]

In addition to these general guidelines, starting in the late 1980's, a system of regulatory impact assessment (RIA) was established. While initially this system covered only financial aspects, its scope was extended step-by-step like in 1999 to possible effects on Austria as a business location or on the Austrian labour market.[22] As of 2013, these different areas have been consolidated within a single law, the *Bundeshaushaltsgesetz* (BHG, BGBl. I Nr. 139/2009).

According to § 17 (1) BHG, the institution drafting a bill has to take into account possible effects on public finances, the national economy, the environment, consumer protection, the law's administrative costs for citizens, different social aspects (like working conditions or the job market) as well as its effect on children and youth or gender equality. The concrete rules concerning how this has to be done are specified in a general decree of the Federal Chancellery, the *WFA-Grundsatz-Verordnung* (WFA-GV, BGBl. II Nr. 489/2012), as well as in a series of more specialized decrees

---

19 Eg. Österreichisches Bundeskanzleramt, *Legistische Richtlinien 1979 Richtlinien zur Gestaltung von Gesetzesvorschriften* (Federal Chancellery of Austria 1979), Österreichisches Bundeskanzleramt, *Handbuch der Rechtssetzungstechnik. Addendum zu Teil 1: Ergänzungen zu den Legistischen Richtlinien 1990 im Zusammenhang mit der Mitgliedschaft der Republik Österreich zur Europäischen Union (EU Addendum)* (Federal Chancellery of Austria 1990); Österreichisches Bundeskanzleramt, *Österreichisches Handbuch 'Bessere Rechtsetzung'* (Federal Chancellery of Austria 2008); circulars GZ BKA 600.824/21-V/2/1980 (29 October 1980); GZ 600.824/1-V/2/81(11 February 1981), 600.824/8-V/A/2/81(9 December 1981), GZ 600.824/8-V/2/98 (13 November 1998), 600.824/0011-V/2/01 (6 March 2001), GZ BKA 600.824/0-V/2/99 (19 February 1999).

20 For an overview, see Österreichisches Bundeskanzleramt, *Standards der Öffentlichkeitsbeteiligung - Empfehlungen für die gute Praxis* (Federal Chancellery of Austria 2009) 14.

21 Österreichisches Bundeskanzleramt 2009, *ibid.*

22 Circular GZ BKA 600.824/0-V/2/99.

for each of the areas.[23] § 9 WFA-GV obliges the lead ministry to start its impact assessment as early as possible and to attach the results to the legislative draft later send out for official public consultations. In addition, the lead ministry is expected to coordinate pro-actively with other ministries as far as the bill might affect areas that fall under their competences.

In sum, there are several guidelines and rules about how legislative drafts should be drafted. Maybe most notably, civil servants are instructed to coordinate with other ministries as early as possible, whenever they expect their proposed draft to have an impact on these other ministries' fields of competence. It is, however, up to them to decide whom they consider to be affected and also the impact assessment is conducted by the ministry itself. The first phase ends with the publication of the ministerial draft (*Ministerialentwurf*).

Once the ministerial draft is published, pre-parliamentary consultations set in. This second phase involves a series of actors like all other ministries, the nine state governments as well as various interest groups and self-regulating bodies (most notably the Social Partners). This procedure is based on historical practice and informal norms, but also on respective stipulations in the laws regulating the activities of the Austrian chambers, professional societies and self-regulating bodies. According to § 93 (2) of the Chamber of Labour Law (*Arbeitskammergesetz*), for example, the chamber has to be consulted on all questions that affect their own interests and affairs. Similar stipulations exist for employers' organisations but also recognised religious groups, amongst others.

Interestingly, none of these laws specifies a clearly defined period that organisations should be granted for their response but only state that the time available should be reasonable (*angemessen*). A circular from the Federal Chancellery's Constitutional Service from 1971, however, stipulates that this period should be at least six weeks 'as a rule'.[24] This period has been restated several times since then.[25]

Vertical consultations are regulated through an agreement between the federal government, the nine regional states and the local level (*Bund-Län-*

---

23 Since 2015 a simplified version of this procedure may be applied in cases where the law's consequences are ex-ante expected not to reach a certain threshold [§ 10a (1) BGBL. II Nr. 67/2015].

24 Circular GZ 53.567-2a/71 (19 July 1971).

25 Eg. circular BKA-600.614/0002-V/2/2008 (2 July 2008).

der-Vereinbarung, BGBl. I Nr. 35/1999). Art. 1 therein stipulates that all ministerial drafts from the federal level have to be submitted to executive bodies on the regional and the local level and postulates a time period of 'at least four weeks' for the latter to submit their statements/opinions. An implementation-circular issued jointly by the Federal Chancellery and the Ministry of Finance (GZ 603.767/1-V/1/99) states that, despite the four weeks clause, again six weeks should be the rule.[26]

Finally, based on a parliamentary resolution from July 5th 1961 and a respective circular of the Federal Chancellery's Constitutional Service, all ministerial drafts as well as respective opinions are to be sent to the federal parliament.[27] Since the early 2000's, all drafts (including attached explanatory memoranda and RIA reports) as well as respective opinions, are then published in a database publicly available via the official parliamentary website. Finally, again based on a parliamentary resolution (200/E XXV.GP.) and a respective circular of the Federal Chancellery,[28] each citizen since 2017 has the opportunity to either submit his/her very own opinion, or to officially express his/her support for opinions already submitted.

In sum, a series of (constitutional) laws, parliamentary resolutions and governmental circulars together constitute a rather dense and transparent system of pre-parliamentary consultations that takes place already *before* the government itself officially discusses, or decides, on the draft. However, a significant part of this system builds on non-binding parliamentary resolutions or ministerial circulars, theoretically leaving ministries with quite some leeway in the process. In addition, when it comes to legally binding provisions like the duty to consult affected bodies, it remains in the responsibility of the ministry and the civil servants in charge with a proposal to decide, which bodies they consider as affected in the first place. After the consultation phase, the ministry in charge may or may not revise the proposal in light of the comments received.

The last step necessary for a ministerial draft to become a government bill (*Regierungsvorlage*), is to pass a vote in the Council of Ministers which is meeting once a week. It lacks formal rules of procedure as all governments so far preferred to keep processes flexible.[29] The big excep-

---

26 Circular GZ 603.767/1-V/1/99 (19 February 1999).
27 Circular GZ 600.614/3-VI/2/76 (14 May 1976).
28 Circular BKA-600.614/0005-V/2/2017 (6 November 2017).
29 WC Müller 'Party Patronage and Party Colonization of the State' in W Crotty and RS Katz (eds), *Handbook of Party Politics* (Sage 2006) 175.

tion here are voting quotas: decisions in the Council of Ministers require a quorum of at least 50 percent of the ministers (with state secretaries having no vote) and adoption requires unanimity. While the quorum is stipulated explicitly in Art. 41 (1) B-VG, the unanimity rule is based on the constitutional principle of individual ministerial responsibility (which requires individual ministers' ability to block decisions), as well as on common law.[30] Once a vote takes place, the Council of Ministers has three options: it may vote in favour of the original draft, adopt a revised version, or reject it.

The drafting and negotiating of governmental bills in practice

Having outlined the institutional framework above, this section will demonstrate, how government bills are drafted in practice. The focus thereby will lie on (a) the role of administrative actors and the relationship between these actors and the political level, and (b) on the coordination within government, that is, amongst different ministers and between coalition parties. Before that, however, two more general mismatches between formal rules and political reality will briefly be addressed.

First, while, according to repeated announcements of the Federal Chancellery, the mandatory pre-parliamentary consultation phase should take six weeks as a rule, this is by far not always the case. While it usually took between six and eight weeks until the mid-1990s, numbers since then dropped to often only three to four weeks.[31] Probably the main reason for this development is a declining interest of today's governments to consider, and take into account, different societal views. Hence, they seek to shorten the time available for critical actors to engage with the proposal and mobilise public resistance.

Just recently, the latest ÖVP-FPÖ government has been repeatedly criticised for again intensifying this development by scholars and members of

---

30 A Pelinka, 'Gesetzgebung in politischen System Österreichs' in W Ismayr (ed), *Gesetzgebung in Westeuropa. EU-Staaten und Europäische Union* (VS-Verlag 2008) 446.

31 H Sickinger 'Parlamentarismus' in E Talos (ed), *Schwarz-Blau. Eine Bilanz des Neu-Regierens* (LIT Verlag 2006) 76.

the opposition.[32] The consultation period of a law modifying the protection of adults,[33] for example, was just ten days instead of six weeks.[34] Regarding law introducing new data-protection rules,[35] in turn, the six-week period was defined in the official documents. However, neither the Council of Ministers nor governing parties in parliament waited for this time to pass. Instead the law passed the National Council more than two weeks before the end of the official consultation phase.[36]

Second, while the clear majority of all bills that in the end turn into law are indeed based on an official government bill (around 70 per cent on average),[37] this is not the only way in which Austrian governments bring their drafts into parliament. Time and again, bills, despite being initiated by the government and elaborated within ministries, enter parliament as private bills brought by (at least five) members of the governing parties. This allows governments to bypass not only the mandatory consultation procedure completely, but also the RIA, and hence allows them to speed up the process significantly.[38] Such 'faked' private bills are often brought in the case of reactive legislation like the transposition of EU law. However, governments fall back to them also when they expect a proposal to meet with significant resistance and hence seek to involve probably critical interest groups as late as possible. According to Schefbeck about one fifth of all laws have been based on private bills over the years.[39]

Again, the latest government provides some nice examples for this strategy. Its coalition-agreement's announcement to partially repeal smoking bans in restaurants met with very harsh criticism not only from the opposition, but also from several other societal actors like medical asso-

---

32 For example, see 'Standortentwicklungsgesetz. Eindruck, dass der Staat auf seine Bürger pfeift' *Kleine Zeitung* (22 August 2018).

33 *Erwachsenenschutz-Anpassungsgesetz*; BGBl. I Nr. 58/2018.

34 Available at https://www.parlament.gv.at/PAKT/VHG/XXVI/ME/ME_00055/index.shtml.

35 *Datenschutz-Anpassungsgesetz 2018*; BGBl. I Nr. 37/2018.

36 Available at https://www.parlament.gv.at/PAKT/VHG/XXV/ME/ME_00322/index.shtml.

37 For example P Biegelbauer and PE Grießler, 'Politische Praktiken von Ministerialbeamt Innen im Österreichischen Gesetzgebungsprozess' (2009) 38 Österreichische Zeitschrift für Politikwissenschaft 64.

38 Pelinka 2008, *ibid*, p. 443.

39 Schefbeck 2006, *ibid*, p. 152.

ciations. The respective legislative draft[40] (therefore?) was brought as a private bill on the 28 February (without any consultations) and passed the National Council within less than one month on 22 March 2018.[41] A law increasing the maximum daily working hours for employees that was harshly criticised especially (but not only) by trade unions, was brought on 14 June and adopted on 5 July 2018.[42]

Administration-government relations

As stated in the previous section, to start working on a ministerial draft, civil servants need an official mandate from their minister. The motivation behind such a mandate may be the minister's personal preferences, strategic (electoral) considerations, recent developments that require (symbolic) reactions, but also coalition agreements, which have become more and more elaborated since the late 1980s.[43] However, in many (about half of the) cases, it is the administration that approaches a minister, calling for a mandate by pointing to areas which, in their view, need (additional) regulation.[44]

Once civil servants have received the official mandate, they face little binding rules with regard to how to draft 'their' laws (see the previous section). In practice, however, several factors help to make sure that clerks indeed seek to act in line with ministers' preferences and that cases, where this (intentionally or unintentionally) may not be the case, do not go unnoticed.

First, a comprehensive system of party-patronage reduces the chance of conflicting interests to occur in the first place. Austria has often been referred to as a prime example for a party-state, where governing parties have been very successful in distributing jobs in the public sector amongst

---

40 *Tabak- und Nichtraucherinnen- bzw. Nichtraucherschutzgesetz*; BGBl. I Nr. 13/2018.
41 Available at https://www.parlament.gv.at/PAKT/VHG/XXVI/A/A_00107/index.sh tml#tab-Uebersicht.
42 Available at https://www.parlament.gv.at/PAKT/VHG/XXVI/A/A_00303/index.sh tml#tab-Uebersicht.
43 WC Müller, 'Koalitionsabkommen in der österreichischen Politik' in G Becker, F Lachmayer and W Oberleitner (eds), *Gesetzgebung zwischen Politik und Bürokratie* (Österreichischer Bundesverlag 1994) 14.
44 Biegelbauer and Mayer 2008, *ibid*, p. 123.

their party fellows.[45] A study comparing the political 'colour' of ministers with the results of staff representation elections in their ministries, for example, showed that in ministerial departments run by the same party for several years, up to 74 percent of the civil servants and employees voted for representatives representing their minister's party.[46] Patronage was especially strong until the 1980s. Studies that are more recent suggest that party influence has weakened somewhat since then and that today it focuses mainly on higher-level positions.[47] However, patronage is far from gone and hence still helps to ensure that civil servants mostly share and pursue similar goals as their respective ministers and/or their ministers' parties.

Ensuring administrative cooperation through patronage works especially well whenever there is little change within ministries with regard to the parties their ministers come from. This was the case basically from 1945 to the late 1990's, when ministries often were led by ministers of the same party for decades. Cooperation may become difficult, however, whenever a ministry, for the first time after a long period, is taken over by a different party and, as a result, faces a potentially 'hostile' bureaucracy. This was the case, for example, in 2000, when the SPÖ, after being in government since 1945 except for only four years, entered opposition and ministers of the ÖVP and the Austrian Freedom Party (FPÖ) were facing ministries like the Ministry of Social Affairs, the Ministry of the Interior or the Ministry of Finance, which had been under social-democratic control for 30 years in a row until then.

In such situations, ministers and their parties seek to redye (*umfärben*) their staff politically as fast as possible. Indeed, the study cited above shows that once a ministry has been taken over and is then run by a minister from a different party for several years, the majorities for the party running the ministry before reduces significantly. It also shows, however, that in the past, this process could take quite long. In 1996, therefore, measures were taken which should reduce the repercussion of previous ministers. For one, top positions like department heads (*Sektionsleiter*), previously

---

45 WC Müller, 'Party Patronage in Austria: Theoretical Considerations and Empirical Findings' in A Pelinka and F Plasser (eds), *The Austrian Party System* (Westview 1989) 327-356; Müller 2006, *ibid*, p. 189.
46 Müller 1989, *ibid.*
47 O Treib, 'Party Patronage in Austria: From Reward to Control in P. Kopecky, P Mair and M Spirova (eds), *Party Patronage and Party Government in European Democracies* (Oxford University Press 2012) 31-53.

hired permanently, since then are given temporary (five-year) contracts only. In addition, tenured officials, when displaced to another position, today are no longer eligible for a position of a similar rank, but only of adequate payment.[48]

Another common strategy applied to deal with 'hostile' clerks has been to (at least partially) disempower them by creating a new position or hierarchical layer above them. The latest ÖVP-FPÖ government, for example, increased the powers of a position labelled 'General Secretary' (*Generalsekretär*) providing it with discretionary power over ministries' department heads. In contrast to most other ministerial jobs, no public tender procedure is required for these positions. Hence, ministers are free to assign them without public advertisement, and without an official selection committee systematically screening and ranking the applicants.

In sum, the Austrian institutional setting provides a variety of possibilities for ministers to put their 'own' people into administration, which helps to reduce conflicts of interest and hence delegation problems between the political and the administrative level in the first place. In addition to this, several factors exist that make delegation-problems unlikely even in cases where interest conflicts – intentionally or unintentionally – may occur.

For one, the size and the activities of ministerial cabinets have increased significantly since the late 1980's, seeking to tighten control over (potentially hostile) ministerial staff.[49] The most important factor, however, is probably the pre-parliamentary consultation procedure. The requirement to send all ministerial drafts to all other ministries as well as to various other stakeholders like interest groups or state governments, combined with the publication of these drafts (and respective opinions) on the parliamentary website makes it highly unlikely that problems, which a legislative draft may cause from the minister's or her government's perspective, will remain undetected. Even in cases, where the government itself

---

48 B Liegl and WC Müller, 'Senior Officials in Austria', in EC Page and V Wright (eds), *Bureaucratic Élites in Western European States* (Oxford University Press 1999) 100.

49 Biegelbauer and Grießler 2009, *ibid*, p. 64; Biegelbauer and Mayer 2008, *ibid.*

fails to detect a potential problem, several 'fire alarms'[50] exist, which are likely to detect, and point the minister/ministry to, these problems.

Civil servants therefore have a huge incentive to anticipate, and take into consideration, potential future reactions when writing a bill. As a result, consultations and coordination with other actors usually set in not only after the first draft has been published, but immediately once the process of writing this draft has started. Being aware that bills in the end not only need the support of their own, but also all other ministers, civil servants actively approach those actors who (a) they consider to provide useful information/knowledge and (b) whose support they expect to be necessary for the proposal to pass the Council of Ministers.[51]

Especially social partners have been playing an important role in this regard. In the past, even the bills themselves were time-and again drafted by, and negotiated between, social partners and brought into parliament by the way of private bills of MPs from governing parties[52] – basically bypassing ministries completely. Within parliament, they usually were adopted without much discussion and/or modification, which brought the social partners the ambivalent reputation of being Austria's shadow government *(Schattenregierung)*. While today this is hardly the case anymore, administrative cooperation with, and coordination between, Austrian social partners and ministries, whenever affected by a bill, is overall still significant. Together with the Ministry of Finance, social partners are usually amongst the very first actors that clerks approach whenever a new law is drafted.[53] And also when lead ministries redraft their bills after the official consultation phase, social partners are regularly consulted.[54]

However, today's amount of involvement of individual social partners depends heavily on the party-political composition of the government. While, for example, employers- and employees organisations both have been consulted quite comprehensively whenever a SPÖ-ÖVP coalition is in power, employees organisations' involvement was significantly lower

---

50 M McCubbins and T Schwartz, 'Congressional Oversight Overlooked: Police Patrols versus Fire Alarms' (1984) 28 American Journal of Political Science 165-179.

51 Biegelbauer and Meyer 2008, *ibid*; Biegelbauer and Grießler 2009, *ibid.*

52 Tálos and Kittel 2001, *ibid*, p. 38.

53 Biegelbauer and Meyer 2008, *ibid.*

54 Tálos and Kittel 2001, *ibid.*

during the first ÖVP-FPÖ coalition from 2006 to 2010,[55] and again has been reported to be rather low for the first months of the latest ÖVP-FPÖ coalition.

Given the strong personnel and ideational overlap between social partners on the one side and SPÖ and ÖVP on the other, this coordination again helps these parties and their ministers not to miss possible detrimental developments in a ministry. It does not work very well for the only other party that has entered government since 1945 – the FPÖ, though. FPÖ's personnel ties with the social partners have been traditionally weak and the party generally has criticised the Austrian social partnership throughout the decades. Consequently, the trend to increase the size of cabinets received a big boost when the FPÖ entered government in 2000 – which significantly reduced the influence of section heads within ministries overall.

In sum, clerks often enjoy quite a lot of freedom and have significant influence on the content of legislation, not least due to their advantages with regard to the technical knowhow compared to ministers and cabinets. Ministers and cabinets do define *ex ante* the general direction to go, but administration has still quite some leeway when deciding what to do precisely. Formal and informal institutional provisions like the mandatory consultation procedure and party-patronage thereby help to assure that administration stays on course without much further action needed.

Whenever problems do occur – e.g. because administration does not share the same goals as the cabinet or the government at large – ministers and cabinets always may take back control, though. This happened, for example, just recently, when the Ministry of Family and Youth Affairs published a bill aiming at indexing the family allowances paid to EU citizens working in Austria taking into consideration the country in which their children live in.[56] This proposal met with harsh criticism due to its expected incompatibility with EU primary law, amongst others, from the Foreign Ministry's Office of International Law, which outlined its concerns in an official opinion published on the parliament's website. Once the government became aware of this, the opinion was recalled immediately and replaced with a more positive one – arguing that the first one was not the correct version and sent out accidentally.

---

55 Tálos 2006, *ibid.*
56 *Familienlastenausgleichsgesetz*; 1/ME XXVI.GP.

Another recent example is a draft on a location development law,[57] which was heavily criticised (amongst others) by environmental groups and constitutional lawyers. Against common practice, the (presumably also critical) Ministry of Environment did not submit its (presumably critical) opinion to parliament (where it would have been publicly available), but directly and unofficially to the ministry in charge. The constitutional service located at the Ministry of Justice did not submit any opinion, arguing that as the draft will be revised thoroughly anyway, comments on the old draft would be unneeded.[58] These examples suggest that not only ministers are able to control the actions of their clerks when necessary, but also are able to suppress (public) criticism from within ministries on their legislative drafts.

In the end, therefore, at least on politicised issues it is the minister/government that decides who is driving the process. Nobody forces the government to take up criticism raised during the consultation phase. In fact, governments' willingness to incorporate the criticism raised in this phase has diminished clearly.[59] And whenever the government expects a bill to meet with too much resistance amongst social partners or other interest groups, it may simply shorten the consultation phase or avoid it, as well as the RIA, altogether by bringing the bill in parliament by the way of a private bill.

Still, drafting legislation works more efficiently, the better the relationship between ministers and their civil servants is. Mechanisms like a bigger cabinet or installing new supervisors certainly help to prevent agency losses. They also make the whole process less effective, though. As a former Minister of Justice from the FPÖ once put it: the more power-conscious a cabinet (has to be), the more difficult the whole process becomes – due to administrative backlashes.[60]

---

57 *Standortentwicklungsgesetz*; 67/ME XXVI. GP.

58 'Standortentwicklungsgesetz: Experten zweifeln an Rechtmäßigkeit' *Die Presse* (4 July 2018).

59 WC Müller, 'Das Regierungssystem' in H Dachs et al (eds), *Politik in Österreich. Das Handbuch* (Manz 2006) 105-118.

60 'Minister kommen und gehen, die Beamten bleiben' *Der Standard* (20 April 2011).

Intra-governmental coordination

When looking at interactions on the political level, i.e. between members of government and coalition parties, again a quite dense network of coordinating routines emerges.

First, ministries responsible for portfolios considered especially important are often allotted with a state secretary coming from a party different from the minister, who keeps an eye on ministerial activities.[61] In the latest ÖVP-FPÖ government, for example, the FPÖ has a state secretary in the ÖVP-run Ministry of Finance and the ÖVP has one in the FPÖ-led Ministry of Interior. In addition, each governing party usually nominates one member of government who has the lead when it comes to coordination with the coalition partner and to whom all other ministers are expected to report their plans and activities. In the SPÖ-ÖVP coalition preceding the latest government all ministers, in addition, were grouped pairwise along the party-cleavage to so-called mirror-ministries (*Spiegelministerien*), which were expected to reconcile their activities amongst each other. This system, however turned out to be too cumbersome and time-consuming and hence was abolished by the latest government.

When issues arise that cannot be solved on lower/administrative levels, *ad hoc* meetings or working groups composed (amongst others) of members of government are called. In addition, there are different regular coordinative meetings that precede the 'official' meeting of the Council of Ministers taking place once a week.[62] While different governments have had their own ways of coordination and hence the precise number and participants of these meetings vary over time, they usually include both meetings *within* governing parties as well as *between* them. Coordination within the latest ÖVP-FPÖ government, for example, starts with weekly inter-party-meetings (usually) on Friday and Monday, which are then followed up by intra-party meetings on Tuesday/the day before the Council. Intra-party meetings take place on three levels: between press officers, between chiefs of cabinets and finally between the parties' ministers responsible for inter-party coordination and their respective teams. Only issues, on

---

61 WC Müller, 'Austria. Tight Coalitions and Stable Government' in WC Müller and K Strøm (eds), *Coalition Governments in Western Europe* (Oxford University Press 2000) 86-125.

62 D Wineroither, *Kanzlermacht-Machtkanzler?: Die Regierung Schüssel im historischen und internationalen Vergleich* (LIT Verlag 2009).

which no compromise has been reached on one level are passed on to the next, higher level.[63]

Notably, participation in these meetings is often not restricted to government representatives, but, depending on the government, may also include representatives of the governing parties' parliamentary groups (like chairmen or thematic spokespersons), as well as other powerful party-stakeholders (like respective state governors or the leaders of important party factions), whose consent is de-facto needed for a party to being able to support a draft.

The Council of Ministers meets once a week, currently every Wednesday. To make it on the agenda, drafts need to arrive at the Federal Chancellery until Thursday, from where they are forwarded to all other ministries. However, if necessary drafts may also be brought in at a later stage (*Tischvorlage*). According to a civil servant working for the Council of Ministers,[64] this happens only on issues where coordination had been concluded informally ex ante, though. Proposals, on which the government fails to solve all conflicts before the official Council of Ministers, usually are taken off the meeting's agenda. As a result, the actual process of voting on the bills in the Council of Ministers in most cases is a mere formality and takes only a few minutes. Hence, actual discussions in the Council of Ministers focus mainly on reviewing concluded projects and on discussing next steps.[65]

There are three main reasons for this system of dense cooperation: First, and as noted above, decisions in the Council of Ministers are taken by unanimity. Hence, it makes little sense for ministers or governing parties to ignore possible concerns of other actors whose support they need anyway. This especially, as the consultation procedure makes it rather unlikely for potential problems to remain undetected.

Second, interest heterogeneity within Austrian governments – and hence the need for coordination – has been quite high throughout the years since 1945. This is, for one, the result of Austria's highly proportional electoral system, which makes single-party governments the exception (see above). In addition, the structure of the Austrian party system has often strongly restricted the choices available for parties when looking for coalition-partners. When Jörg Haider took the lead on the FPÖ in 1986

---

63 Phone interview with the Austrian government spokesman, 10 September 2018.
64 Phone interview with a member of the Ministerratsdienst, 27 August 2018.
65 Phone interview with the Austrian government spokesman, 10 September 2018.

and subsequently turned it into a radical-right populist party, the other Austrian parties decided to form a *cordon sanitaire*, and refused to form a coalition with the FPÖ. Given the FPÖ's electoral success in the coming years, however, neither centre-left, nor a centre-right coalitions excluding the FPÖ were possible as of then. Hence, a *grand coalition* between centre-left SPÖ and centre-right ÖVP (holding quite different views on many issues) was de facto the only option that provided a government with a parliamentary majority. This situation changed only in 2000, when the ÖVP left the cordon sanitaire and entered a coalition with the FPÖ. But even within this coalition, interest heterogeneity was large on many issues.

Finally, as an aftermath to the fierce societal conflict in the inter-war period, which led to the civil war in 1934 and where the predecessor parties of SPÖ and ÖVP faced each other on different sides, the general level of mistrust between these two parties has been high also after 1945. While the experiences of the Second World War led both camps to acknowledge that peaceful cooperation (and a consociational system) was the only way to go, both parties therefore were still very conscious to know what the other side was doing.

The fate of governmental bills

Austria's first federal parliamentary chamber, the National Council, has traditionally considered itself as being a working parliament like the German *Bundestag* rather than as a talking shop like the British *House of Commons*.[66] Hence, instead of being merely a body where governing- and opposition parties seek to publicly communicate their different views to the electorate, the Austrian National Council raises the claim to play an active part in the process of law-making.[67] In day-to-day praxis, however, the legitimizing function clearly dominates[68] and the actual role of parliament when it comes to legislation is comparatively weak for three reasons: First, decision-making in Austria after the Second World War was dominated by consocialism and neo-corporatism (see above). As a result, time and again important decisions were negotiated outside parliament between

---

66 The Federal Council plays a subordinated role only as, in most cases, it can only delay legislation. Hence, this section focuses on the National Council only.
67 Sickinger 2006, *ibid*, p. 48.
68 Schefbeck 2006, *ibid*, p. 150.

social partners, and only 'nodded trough' in the National Council. Second, parliament's resources have been quite limited, both in terms of parliamentary administration and the resources available to parliamentarians themselves. Third, an electoral system dominated by party lists makes parliamentarians heavily reliant on their own party to get re-elected. This makes criticising the government a risky undertaking for parliamentarians from the governing parties.

As a result, it comes as no surprise that according to parliamentary statistics, only a negligible share of government bills (around 5 percent between 1996 and 2018) that entered parliament have subsequently failed to turn into law.[69] This is not to say that most government bills pass the parliament without any changes, though. According to Schefbeck,[70] the share of government bills adopted without any changes varies between 31.2 and 63.1 per cent between 1966 and 2004.[71]

In the majority of cases, changes are made on the committee level. However, the share of changes adopted in the plenary (i.e. at the latest moment possible) has consequently risen over the years from 25 per cent in the legislative period from 1996 to 1999 to about 43 per cent in the last legislative period from 2013 to 2017. This suggests that, like for the pre-parliamentary phase, the speed of decision-making has increased over time, and that informal bodies like negotiating teams consisting out of members of parliament from the governing parties, representatives of ministries and interest groups, have increased their importance compared to official parliamentary procedures like committee meetings.[72] As a result, and in line with a decrease of interest-group involvement at the pre-parliamentary stage, the involvement of opposition parties within parliament into legislative processes has decreased over time.

---

69 Numbers and following data kindly provided by the Austrian parliamentary directorate.
70 Schefbeck 2006, *ibid*, p. 152.
71 From the data available it is of course not possible to estimate the amount of changes that government bills usually changes – i.e. to what extent amendments concern only small details or significantly affect the overall content of the bills.
72 See also Schefbeck 2006, *ibid*, p. 153.

Conclusion

A daily newspaper recently compared government-administration relations in Austria with a modern airplane – which describes the general situation quite nicely: for long periods, when the weather is nice, autopilot
mode is running. While ministers and their cabinets define the general di-
rections to go, civil servants within ministries do enjoy quite some freedom and, due to their technical knowhow, may have significant influence
on the precise content of legislation. Whenever the weather becomes ruff
due to inter-governmental disagreements or the politicisation of the draft,
however, autopilot is turned off. Ministers and cabinets take over control
and the room for manoeuvre of civil servants becomes significantly nar-
rower.[73]

With regard to coordination *within* governments and administration (i.e.
between different ministries), there are only few mandatory rules that actors have to follow. However, institutional provisions like the requirement
for unanimity in the Council of Ministers or the system of comprehensive
pre-parliamentary consultations ensure that coordination is rather dense
nevertheless. For both levels, far-reaching informal routines have been established. The positive aspect of these routines is that they may be adapted
flexibly to fit current needs. Their downside is a lack of public transparency, which sometimes makes it difficult for third actors to trace how and
why specific decisions are taken or certain compromises are reached.

Looking at developments over time, two changes stand out. First, due to
a high level of party patronage combined with an increased frequency of
changes in the party-political composition of governments since the early
2000's, ministers today are more often confronted with civil servants hired
by ministers from other parties and hence potentially holding quite different political views. As a result, government-administration relations today,
on average, are less harmonious than they were in earlier decades. In reac-
tion, new control mechanisms (like bigger cabinets) have been introduced.
While, thanks to this, control still seems to work quite fine, the mere fact
that stricter control is needed makes legislative processes running less
smooth than in the past or in ministries, where interest heterogeneity is
still low.

---

73 Der Standard 2011, *ibid.*

Second, Austria's steady move from a consensus-democracy to a more conflict oriented political system since the 1980's also had its impact on the way government bills are drafted. Governments' willingness to take into account the views or the critique raised by other parties or interest groups from 'opposing' fronts has diminished considerable – especially at times when the SPÖ (and hence the party with strong ideological and personal links to Austrian employee-organisations) has not been a member of government.

In addition, the time provided for mandatory public consultations has structurally declined, and time and again governments avoid them all together by falling back to 'faked' private bills instead of official government bills. Hence, while the Austrian institutional setting still stimulates comprehensive coordination *within* the executive level, it at the same time allows governments to keep this coordination largely behind closed doors and to 'lock out' external actors from participating in the process – and, by doing so, to circumvent public debates and hence to shield themselves from public scrutiny or possible (opposition) critique in the process.

The Czech Republic

Marian Kokeš

Introduction

The Constitutional Court of the Czech Republic describes 'good law' as law that is "necessary, effective, clear, coherent and accessible."[1] Generally, processes by which legislation is created and prepared by the government and subsequently scrutinized and enacted by the parliament are key to ensuring that new law meets these criteria. But as the Constitutional Court also stated: "Art. 1 (1) of the Czech Constitution, which describes the Czech Republic as a democratic rule of law state established on respect for rights and freedoms of a man and citizen, includes a normative principle of a democratic rule of law state. Respect for the same purpose is also reflected in Art. 2 (3) of the of the Czech Constitution, pursuant to which state power may be asserted only in cases, within the bounds, and in the manner provided for by law."[2] This implies that even parliament cannot proceed when adopting laws (statutes) in an arbitrary manner but are bound by law - sources of the parliamentary law that contained (not only) the rules of the legislative process.

Unfortunately, the current state of law-making and legal order in general in the Czech Republic does not correspond with the constitutional principles and rules for the creation of harmonious, clear and comprehensible law. This rather skeptical statement could create a context in which will be this chapter - analyzing role of the government in the legislative process (in its wider sense) in the Czech Republic, especially in its preparatory phase or within its two first stages (initiation and drafting) - placed. It must be said that due to those deficiencies a process of law-making is for a

---

1 Judgment no. Pl. US 77/06, English version at https://www.usoud.cz/en/decisions/.
2 Judgment no. Pl. US 55/10, English version at https://www.usoud.cz/en/decisions/.

long time criticized by legal theory[3] and also by the judiciary, including the Czech Constitutional Court.[4]

Overview of the constitutional and political system

According to Art. 1 (1) of the Constitution,[5] the Czech Republic is a unitary and democratic state governed by the rule of law. Despite the fact that these principles have recently been weakened due to a number of factors (e.g. efforts to strengthen direct democracy, constitutional anchoring of direct election of the president and efforts to strengthen his influence within the executive power), the political system of the Czech Republic could be defined as a parliamentary democracy based on the division of powers, with directly elected president as the head of state, with dominant role of the government as the highest body of executive power and bicameral parliament that consists of the Chamber of Deputies (lower chamber, 200 members) and the Senate (upper chamber, 81 members).

The government consists of the prime minister, deputy prime ministers, and ministers. The president shall appoint the prime minister and, based on her proposal, the other members of the government and entrusts them with the management of the ministries (or other offices). The government acts as a collective body, formally headed by the prime minister. The prime minister organizes activities of the government, heads its meetings and acts on its behalf. Her privileged position consists of proposing other members of the government for appointment to the president and proposing their dismissal. According to the Constitution, position of the prime

---

3 Research on law-making remains largely neglected in the Czech Republic. In general attention of legal theory has long been primarily focused on the issues of interpretation and application of the law by courts (adjudication), which by far does not correspond with the complexity and importance of law-making in the process of legal regulation; see further M Kokeš, 'Teorie zákonodárství aneb pokus čelit nezájmu právní teorie a politologie o legislativní tvorbu práva v ČR' (2016) 49 Správní právo (Legislativní příloha) I-XXXIX.

4 See further J Kysela 'The Influence of the Constitutional Court on the Rules of Legislative Process in the Czech Republic' (2014) Prague Law Working Papers Series II/4, Prague: Charles University, also available at: http://ssrn.com/abstract=254056 5.

5 Constitutional Act no. 1/1993 Coll., English translation at http://www.psp.cz/en/doc s/laws/constitution.html.

minister is however not dominant and formally she has no opportunity to intervene into activities of individual ministries. Yet the prime minister is usually also a leader of the strongest political party and because she is primarily responsible for recruiting ministers from her party, at least these ministers are under strong informal pressure from the prime minister.

Position of the prime minister and the government as a whole in the Czech political system, however, is influenced by other factors, especially by a distribution of power within coalition government. Due to a proportional electoral system set for elections to the Chamber of Deputies, (two-, three -, or four- party) coalition governments have been a typical feature for most of the time since establishment of the Czech Republic in 1993. Hence, governing usually requires a compromise between parties participating in coalition, but such achievement is not easy in Czech reality of multi-party political system, especially in last decade where traditional political parties are gradually replaced by new political entities often inclined to populism (Hnutí ANO, SPD, Piráti). Moreover, election results often create stalemate situations and appointed governments have fragile support in the Chamber of Deputies to which the government is responsible. This relationship is reflected in the Constitution both during the process of formation of a new government[6] and afterwards through the possibility of the Chamber of Deputies to dismiss the government by approving a resolution of no confidence in that government (Art. 72). To adopt this resolution, an absolute majority of all deputies (i. e. minimum 101) must give their consent. The relationship between the Chamber of Deputies and the government enshrined in the Constitution also indirectly defines relationship between the two chambers of the parliament. The Chamber of Deputies is a stronger chamber in relation to the government while the Senate has no direct links with the government.

Therefore it can be stated that coalition governments in the Czech Republic are not very stable ("permanent struggle for 101 deputies").[7] Thus, political conflicts arise not only between majority and minority (govern-

---

6 According to Art. 68 (3) of the Constitution, within thirty days of its appointment, the government shall go before the Chamber of Deputies and ask it for a vote of confidence.

7 It should be noted that several governments have collapsed also due to political scandals, e.g. governments of Prime Minister Topolánek (2009) or Prime Minister Nečas (2013). See P Kolář, J Kysela, J Syllová, J Georgiev and J Pecháček, *Parlament České republiky* (Leges 2013).

ment and parliamentary opposition), but also inside governing coalition (between political parties participating in coalition). From the point of view of law-making, feature of the former is that instead of seeking consensus on the content of the new legislation (law), it is often enforced through a majority-based decision making, in some cases even at the cost of violating the right of parliamentary opposition.[8] Feature of the latter is not only a difficult way to achieve a compromise over governmental agenda, even with regard to the different programs and interests of political parties participating in the coalition, but also promoting its own political agenda and goals often at the expense of the coalition partner in an effort to gain political popularity and a dominant role within the government.

In addition, it should be stressed that since 2013 the Constitution has introduced the direct election of the president, which in fact strengthened his political influence (but without changing his powers), through which the president has increasingly intervened into activities of the government (especially in personnel matters).

All abovementioned features weaken the government's position in the Czech political system.[9] It is obvious that in a situation where the government relies on fragile support in the Chamber of Deputies and where within the coalition fundamental political disputes arise, willingness of the government to set key political issues and (among others) to take unpopular but necessary measures through legal regulation to enforce its own policies and promised political reforms will not be large. And even if the willingness is high, such government will not have enough "political capital" to enforce them in the parliament. Nevertheless, the government still has a dominant position within the executive power, as well as being a dominant actor within the law-making process. In other words, the maxim that the government, supported by ministerial bureaucracy and equipped with strong agenda control, is the central legislative actor., is valid also in the Czech Republic.[10]

---

8 Judgment no. Pl. US 55/10, for English version see https://www.usoud.cz/en/decis ions/.
9 See J Kysela and M Kokeš, 'Role vlády v procesu právotvorby v České republice se zřetelem k efektivitě vládnutí' (2018) 51 Správní právo (Legislativní příloha) XC-CVIII.
10 See H Döring, 'Time as a Scarce Resource: government Control of the Agenda' in H Döring (ed) *parliaments and Majority Rule in Western Europe* (Campus/St. Martin's Press 1995) 223–246.

Legal and institutional framework of the law-making process

Law-making process (in its narrow sense) is defined as formal and by law regulated process of law-making by the legislator which is initiated by the formal submission of a legislative proposal (the draft), i.e. through exercise of the right of legislative initiative, and ends with the promulgation of the law.[11] Thus it is a multi-step process formally regulated by law. Legislative process in a wider sense absorbs also another stages or phases of legislating. For a definition we could use a concept of *"regulatory cycle of legislation"* presented by prof. U. Karpen, who defined the following main steps (phases) of legislative process: a) impulse, b) analysis of the problem, c) policy-setting, d) definition of the targets and instruments of regulation, e) drafting, f) deliberation and adoption of the draft in parliament, g) implementing, h) monitoring of implementation and finally i) amendment (if necessary) in a new procedure.[12] In short, there are four phases of legislating: initiative and drafting, deliberation and adoption, implementation and enforcement, control and amendment.[13] From the perspective of formal (normative) framework it should be added, however, that legal regulation of legislative process in the Czech Republic by sources of parliamentary law reflects primarily its narrow sense, so the mentioned „*deliberation and adoption in parliament"* phase.

As in most countries the basic structure of the legislative process in the Czech Republic is part of the Constitution, primarily in its Chapter Two called "Legislative power" (Art. 15-53). According to Art. 15 of the Constitution the legislative power of the Czech Republic is vested in the parliament.[14] There are various sources of parliamentary law that include beside the Constitution also the rules of procedure of both chambers of par-

---

11 See P Badura, *Staatsrecht: systematische Erläuterung des Grundgesetzes für die Bundesrepublik Deutschland* (C.H. Beck 2003) 535, or J Filip *Vybrané kapitoly ke studiu ústavního práva* (Masarykova univerzita 2001) 276.

12 See U Karpen, 'Comparative Law: Perspectives of Legislation' (2012) 6 Legisprudence 149–189.

13 See also C Stefanou, 'Drafters, Drafting and the Policy Process' in C Stefanou and H Xanthaki (eds) *Drafting legislation: a modern approach* (Ashgate 2008) 321–334.

14 The Constitution does not preclude a possibility that direct democratic procedures (such as a state referendum) could be used as initiative for the adoption of laws.

liament[15]; more detailed rules of conduct as adopted by resolutions of the individual chambers of parliament on the basis of § 1 (2) of their rules of procedure (so called "autonomous resolution"); as well as settled practice of parliamentary chamber and its bodies, which can be considered part of the legislative process owing to their long-term repetition – these "unwritten rules" are capable of solving issues explicitly unregulated by the rules of procedure and optimize the self-organization of parliament. The last three sources of parliamentary law are the expression of autonomy of parliament. These rules are to a certain extent necessary, since the Constitution naturally regulates the rules of legislative process merely in general manner and anticipates adoption of more detailed rules. In sum, basic framework of the law-making process is set out in the Constitution, details of internal procedures of relevant actors related to the process are prescribed at the statutory level.

Legal framework of the two first stages of the legislative process (in its wider sense), i.e. initiation and drafting, is strongly underdeveloped. Basically the only relevant legal norm are the Legislative Rules of the Government (further as the Legislative Rules) adopted by the resolution of the government.[16] The Legislative Rules define their main purpose and subject matter by regulating procedure of the ministries and other central state administration bodies in the drafting and negotiation of the proposals of legislation, as well as defining the requirements of the content and form of the bill (i.e. legislative technics). The Legislative Rules originally used to regulate also activities of the Legislative Council of the Government and its working groups, but recently these issues were transferred to the Statute of the Legislative Council and to the Rules of Procedure of the Legislative Council (see below).

Every proposal (draft) of a bill must be presented firstly to the Chamber of Deputies (through its Chairperson and the Organizing/Steering Committee). Art. 41 (2) of the Constitution confers the right of legislative initiative to following bodies: a deputy (!); a group of deputies (however

---

15 Act no. 90/1995 Coll. (Rules of Procedure of the Chamber of Deputies), English translation at https://www.psp.cz/en/docs/laws/1995/90_index.html, and Act no. 107/1999 Coll. (Rules of Procedure of the Senate), English translation at https://www.senat.cz/informace/zakon106/zakony/zak107-eng.php.

16 Adopted by the 19 March 1998 government Resolution No. 188. at https://www.vlada.cz/cz/ppov/lrv/dokumenty/legislativni-pravidla-vlady-91209/.

formed and however large); the Senate (as a whole); a council of regional administrations and, of course, the government.

The ordinary legislative process is usually divided into three stages (so called "readings") in each chamber of the parliament where proposed bills are discussed (on plenary session and also in committees), (often) amended (in the second and third readings) and voted upon. If the Chamber of Deputies expresses after the third reading consent with a proposed bill (including amendments approved by deputies), the bill is forwarded to the Senate for its approval. In this context, it is necessary to emphasize that the Senate has much weaker legislative power than the Chamber of Deputies.[17]

If the Senate rejects the proposed bill, the Chamber of Deputies shall vote on it again and the proposed bill is adopted if it is approved by an absolute majority of all deputies (min. 101 votes). If the Senate returns the proposed bill to the Chamber of Deputies with proposed amendments, the Chamber of Deputies shall vote on the version of the bill approved by the Senate and the proposed bill is adopted by its resolution, but if the Chamber of Deputies does not approve the version of the proposed bill adopted by the Senate, it shall vote again on the version it submitted to the Senate. The proposed bill is adopted if it is approved by an absolute majority of all deputies, too. Thus, within the ordinary legislative process[18] the Chamber of Deputies has always the last word and opinion (resolution) of the Senate could be overruled by an absolute majority of all deputies.

At the end of the legislative process the president must sign the approved bill, but (with the exception of constitutional laws), the president may refuse to sign it because she has the right to return adopted bill (Art. 50 of the Constitution). The Chamber of Deputies alone (not the Senate) shall vote on whether to uphold the adopted bill. If the Chamber of Deputies reaffirms its approval of the bill by an absolute majority of all deputies, the bill shall be promulgated in the Collection of Laws, otherwise the bill shall be deemed not to have been adopted.

---

17 See J Kysela, *Dvoukomorové systémy: teorie, historie a srovnání dvoukomorových parlamentů* (Eurolex Bohemia 2004).

18 Within the legislative process on proposals of constitutional bills or bills according to Art. 40 of the Constitution (especially an electoral law), it is necessary to approve them by both chambers of the parliament, so the Chamber of Deputies does not have the right to overrule the Senate.

It should be added that through a norm control proceeding under Art. 87 (1) (a) of the Constitution [in the sense of the provisions of § 68 (2) of the Act on the Constitutional Court],[19] the Constitutional Court holds a task to assess if the content of laws is compatible with the constitutional order and review whether the bill was adopted and issued within the confines of the powers set down in the Constitution, and further whether it was issued in the constitutionally-prescribed manner. The Constitutional Court's has had strong influence on the form of law-making process through its case-law based on development of the rule of law as a concept of limiting the legislature – not the limits of the content of laws, but limits of the ways in which laws are created.[20]

Role of the government in preparatory phase of legislative process

The government has an enormous influence on the law-making process because the vast majority of laws (bills) is initiated and drafted by the executive. Among abovementioned bodies with the right of legislative initiative, the government, not surprisingly, is dominant, but initiatives by single deputies or group of deputies are not inconsiderable (not only from the statistical point of view). An average proportion of the government proposals of bills in total number of initiatives on average slightly exceeds 50 percent.[21] This number is significantly lower than in many Western European countries,[22] but almost all important or complex laws are submitted by the government.

Let's move our attention to preparatory phase of the legislative process (i.e. initiation and drafting stages) and try to answer questions about organizing the policy agenda and then preparing legislative proposals (bills) by

---

19 Act no. 182/1993 Coll. (Act on the Constitutional Court), English translation at https://www.usoud.cz/en/legal-basis/.

20 See further Kysela 2014, *ibid.*

21 In 2006-2010 election term the government submitted 314 out of 613 proposed bills (51 percent), in 2010-2013 it was 347 out of 621 (56 percent), and in 2013-2017 it was 376 out of 644 (58 percent). Data extracted from the Chamber of Deputies webpage, available at http://public.psp.cz/en/sqw/sntisk.sqw.

22 See D Olson and DM Norton, 'Legislatures in Democratic Transition' in D Olson and DM Norton (eds), *The New parliaments of Central and Eastern Europe* (Frank Cass 1996) 1–15, or SM Saiegh, 'Lawmaking' in S Martin, T Saalfeld and KW Ström (eds), *The Oxford Handbook of Legislative Studies* (OUP 2014) 484.

the government. It is obvious that the drafting process is a part of the legislative process, which in turn is part of the policy process. Thus, the bill is first and foremost the legal expression of a policy developed within the government or particular ministry. Thus, the first step in the drafting legislation must be a political directive of government (policy-setting). Such a political directive reacts to a problem-impulse, wherever this originates. But if we put this statement within the context of coalition government, we could stressed upon some specific problematic features connected with the coalition government in the Czech Republic that occur also within the legislative process, especially in its preparatory phase.

Initiation stage

As it was indicated earlier in the Czech political system (due to proportional electoral system) the coalition governments are unavoidable and there is a dominant dichotomy of the government and the opposition that comes with strong political party conflict. It inherently demands cooperation and compromise by parties with divergent policy goals to reach a consensus on that political issue. As S. Burkhart and M. Lehnert stated, "emphasis on consensual politics and policy outcomes sometimes obscures the fact that consensus and cooperation are conditional: although most policy outcomes are highly consensual, the road to achieving such outcomes is often paved with severe conflicts arising, for example, from inter- and intra-party competition, struggles between government and opposition or between the two parliamentary chambers."[23] This statement of course applies also within law making process, legislation, especially in its initiation (policy agenda setting) and drafting stage that is always a challenge for coalition governments. It is obvious that within the coalition government participating political parties, in the pursuit of their own interests, should have the incentives to seek, and the means to secure a policy agenda that accommodates (inasmuch as possible) the preferences of all partners in the coalition. But if the coalition is incoherent and instable, political parties participating in the government tend to prioritize different poli-

---

23 See S Burkhart and M Lehnert, 'Between Consensus and Conflict: Law-Making Processes in Germany' (2008) 17 German Politics 223-231.

cy agenda and take conflicting positions on these political issues and enforce and introduce only their own favourable policies.[24]

Another problematic feature connected with the preparatory phase of law-making process in the Czech Republic is an absence of legislative conception, i. e. changes of law are isolated, made often automatically (discontinuously with the previous government) as a result of a change in the government without a more comprehensive legislative conception ("we are bringing a change because we have promised changes to our voters"). We could speak about "pro-regulative obsession" of each government created in the Czech Republic. It is obvious that legislation is an essential tool for government to achieve its policy aims, but it should be only used as a solution where every other regulatory choice would not be effective. But problem occurs when the government as its own policy aims sets "policy of change" that is necessarily accompanied by massive legislative changes („the government must be seen to have done something"). In the Czech Republic it is true not only for primary legislation (laws),[25] but also for secondary legislation (especially governmental regulations[26] or ministerial ordinances[27]). In relation to laws the overall number of new laws does not increase, but there is a trend of increasing number of laws that amend the existing laws, often very shortly after the latter were enacted.[28]

---

24 In recent years, it is not uncommon in the Czech Republic that political parties participating in the government coalition raise political conflicts among themselves based on seek to gain positive political points for government successes and, conversely, to blame their coalition partner for failure. For example, participation of the Social Democratic Party (ČSSD) in the government coalition with populist party ANO has been seen as a key reason for its declining electoral preferences, while the preferences of the latter party have grown.

25 Data from R Zbíral, 'Legislative process in the Czech Republic' in H Xanthaki and U Karpen (eds) *Legislation in European Countries* (Hart, in print).

26 The government is entitled to issue regulations in order to implement laws; regulations shall at the same time remain within the bounds of the given laws (Art. 78 of the Constitution).

27 The ministries are entitled by the Art. 79 (3) of the Constitution to issue ordinances if they are authorized to do that by a law, if they remain within the bounds of the given law and if the law explicitly contains a provision authorizing issuance of the given ordinance.

28 See F Cvrček et al., *Legislativa: Teoretická východiska a problémy* (Aleš Čeněk 2017).

Someone could object that the government annually adopts (by the governmental resolution) the Plan of Legislative Tasks of the Government, based on the coalition agreement, the governmental programme and the Outlook of Legislative Works prepared for the whole election period (four years).[29] Nevertheless we could hardly speak about unified legislative conception. In fact, the Plan of Legislative Tasks of the government is rather a set of proposals proposed by individual ministries, so it is a summary of each departmental legislative plans and a list of titles of legislative drafts to be submitted to the government or to the parliament for the given year. From this list, however, it is usually not possible to identify something about the content of bills and therefore to evaluate their necessity and effectiveness or their relationship to other parts of the legal order.[30] Problem lies in the fact that at the executive level, there is an absence of a body that would coordinate legislative works within the government, provide unifying principles in the preparatory phase of the legislative process and deal with legislative activities of the government in a comprehensive manner.

Thus, for searching the construction of the policy agenda in the Czech Republic it is necessary to go one floor below within the executive, from the government to individual ministries and their departments. Each minister controls a single government department, which normally has jurisdiction over a single policy area. Each ministry has its own legislative department responsible for legislative drafting which, under the supervision of the directing minister, act as "the key agent for the preparation and development of policy coming to the government."[31] The abovementioned absence of a body responsible for coordination of legislative activities within the government thus causes that each ministry has its own approach for legislative activities and its "own" legislation as an essential tool for

---

29 Available at https://www.vlada.cz/cz/media-centrum/dulezite-dokumenty/plan-legi slativnich-praci-vlady-na-rok-2019-170977/.

30 See J Vedral, 'K příčinám nynějšího stavu právního řádu a k možnostem vlády při jeho (re)formování' in A Gerloch and J Kysela (eds), *Tvorba práva v České republice po vstupu do Evropské unie* (ASPI 2007) 87–103.

31 See M Burch, Organizing the Flow of Business in Western European Cabinets. In J Blondel and F Müller-Rommel (eds), *Governing Together* (Macmillan 1993) 99–130.

achieving its own policy aims.[32] Another problem is that it is hard to learn something about existence of political directives or instructions for drafting, despite the obvious need to have such rules in order to ensure that the bill is adequately scrutinized. If there are no such instructions or are only vague, many of the basic choices end up in the hands of the drafters alone and this feature means that the drafting can develop non-transparently in a political vacuum. As M. Laver and K. A. Shepsle stated, which is also relevant for describing situation in the Czech Republic, "given the intense pressure of work and lack of access to civil service specialists in other departments, it seems unlikely that cabinet ministers will be able successfully to poke their noses very deeply into the jurisdictions of their cabinet colleagues. This implies that members of the cabinet will have only very limited ability to shape the substance of policy emanating from the department of a ministerial colleague (...) Ministerial discretion is sustained, principally but not exclusively, by the control over the policy agenda that each minister exercises in his or her own departmental jurisdiction."[33]

The discussed lack of civil service specialists[34] causes another problematic feature of drafting bills, namely the delegation of drafting works outside ministries or the government to special ad hoc expert committees (often composed also by judges)[35] or even to private entities (law firms) with their own particular vision on content and form of legal regulation.[36]

---

32 See J Vedral 2007, *ibid.,* p. 99-100, or M Škop and B Vacková, 'Být legislativcem: Empirická šetření v administrativních fázích legislativy' (2019) 27 Časopis pro právní vědu a praxi 5-28.

33 See M Laver and KM Shepsle, *Making and Breaking governments* (Cambridge University Press 1996) 31-32.

34 According to the Act no. 234/2014 Coll. (Act on Civil Service) and the governmental Regulation no. 106/2015 Coll. (On Categories of Civil Service), all civil servants employed and categorized within category "Legislation and legal service" shall have special knowledge and skills of legislative drafting.

35 For example, expert committees for preparation of drafting new Civil Code (Act no. 89/2012 Coll.) or new Penal Order.

36 For example, preparation of drafting new Act on Building Regulation (Act no. 183/2006 Coll).

Drafting and negotiating stage

The process of drafting (adopting) bills within the executive that is formalized by the Legislative Rules suffers from some problematic features. Many scholars in the Czech Republic dispute legal character of the Legislative Rules because of their subordinate character.[37] According to § 21 of the Competence Act,[38] governmental resolutions are binding to the government itself, to all ministries and also other state administration bodies. Thus, through the Legislative Rules in the form of a government resolution, the government can regulate legislative drafting of all ministries as well as of other state administration bodies. On the other hand, the Legislative Rules are not binding to other subjects with the right of legislative initiative, even as regards the formal requirements for the content of the draft.[39]

The drafting process is regulated as a multi-step procedure, so every drafted bill has to overstep formal (procedural) hurdles. According to the Legislative Rules a first version of the bill are drafted by the ministry responsible for the given field of regulation, each bill has to meet formal and substantive (legislative technics) requirements (something like "guidelines for legislation") enshrined in the Legislative Rules (Art. 25-60). All drafted bills have to be accompanied by explanatory report (Art. 9 of the Legislative Rules) divided into a general part and a specific part that obligatorily contains: summary of drafted law, evaluation of its accordance with the constitutional and legal order, international treaties and the EU law, cost-benefit analysis, risk evaluation on corruption and dangers for privacy and personal data, followed by explanation of each provision of the bill. Al-

---

37 See J Wintr, *Česká parlamentní kultura* (Auditorium 2010) 43, or J Filip, 'K postavení Legislativní rady vlády České republiky' (2007) 15 Časopis pro právní vědu a praxi 203.

38 Act no. 2/1969 Coll (on the Establishment of Ministries and other Central Bodies of State Administration of the Czech Republic – Competence Act).

39 Moreover, the Constitutional Court declared that the violation of Legislative Rules without a violation of the competence prescribed by the Constitution or by the laws does not give rise to grounds for derogation due to a failure to observe the constitutionally prescribed manner of the legislative process. In practice, certain parts of the Legislative Rules are generally respected by other subjects as well, but, unfortunately, quite often there are also situations in which the government itself does not respect its own Legislative Rules; see judgment Pl. ÚS 24/07 of 31 January 2008.

though the content of explanatory reports is often used by judiciary as an interpretative tool for searching original intention of the legislative drafter, its content quality is often criticized because it is not detailed enough, sometimes containing more political declarations than a detailed analysis of legal regulation.

Almost all drafted bills shall be also accompanied RIA report, i.e. ex ante review of social-economic impact of legislation.[40] Although the original meaning of this tool lies in evaluation of impact of intended legal regulation and thus should be made before a decision about preparing legal regulation is made and the bill drafted, this is hardly the case in the Czech Republic. First of all, there are numerous cases when RIA is not performed at all, based on the exceptions granted to individual bills by the decision of the chairman of the Legislative Council of the Government. Another problem lies in the fact that RIA verdict is only recommendatory, so in practice it is often respected neither by the government nor the parliament. The lack of experts preparing RIA causes low quality of the evaluations.[41]

The bill, including the explanatory report and (if available) RIA report, is then sent by the drafting ministry to other ministries and public bodies[42] for consultations.[43] The process of consultations is in practice very often and to a large extent used for proposing significant changes to the proposed bill, especially by other ministries. Therefore, it is not uncommon that after this the drafting process of the bill is terminated or postponed because received comments have to be implemented or negotiated by the drafting ministry.

After that the drafted bill proceeds to the Legislative Council of the Government and its working groups. The Legislative Council is an adviso-

---

40 The RIA guidelines provide a detailed methodology how to calculate cost and benefits of possible solutions to the problem and how to rank the solutions. The first general guidelines of RIA in the Czech Republic were adopted in 2007, latest RIA guidelines have been in force since 2016; all are available at https://ria.vlada.cz/.

41 Institutional framework is formed by the Section on RIA located within the Office of the Government and Working Group for RIA within the Legislative Council of the Government, composed of experts mainly from academia.

42 E.g. courts, the Ombudsman, other state bodies, universities.

43 From a technical point of view, communication is primarily made online via electronic library *eKLEP* where all necessary documents for drafting process are preserved; eKLEP is available at https://apps.odok.cz/eklep.

ry body of the government. Its members (primarily legal scholars or other legal professions)[44] are named by the government and headed (usually) by the Minister of Justice. Competences and tasks of the Legislative Council and its (nine) working groups, defined by the Statute of the Legislative Council and to the Rules of Procedure of the Legislative Council, are to review and evaluate all legislative drafts submitted to the government,[45] especially if they are compatible with the constitutional and legal order, international treaties and EU law. The Legislative Council also review whether the drafts are necessary and if their content is clearly formulated and structured. Although opinions of the Legislative Council have also recommendatory character, in practice the positive outcome of the review is generally taken as a condition for submission of the bill to the governments meeting.[46] The Legislative Council has therefore became an important body in the law-making within the executive phase. However, if the expert opinions get into conflict with political interests of ministries or the government, the positions of the latter subjects usually prevail. One of the alternatives how to circumvent the negative view of the Legislative Council is to submit the proposal through the legislative initiative by friendly deputies in the Chamber of Deputies.[47]

The final (modified) version of the drafted bill is than submitted for approval to the government on its meeting where is formally voted upon and in case of consent sent to Chairperson of the Chamber of Deputies for starting the legislative process in the parliament (see above).

---

44 The Legislative Council has approximately 30 members.
45 Approximately 350 legislative proposals (i.e. bills, governmental regulations, ministerial ordinances) per year are reviewed. The working groups structured along their legal specialization (e.g. on penal law, administrative law, EU law) review especially proposals of ministerial ordinances. The Legislative Council itself reviews mainly the bills (of laws), but only the most important ones are discussed on the session of the Legislative Council (about 30 to 90 per year).
46 The Legislative Council may either recommend the bill for adoption by the government or recommend substantial changes and amendments in the draft, it may also recommend rejection of the bill.
47 See Filip 2007, *ibid*, p. 203, or Vedral 2007, *ibid*, p. 99.

Marian Kokeš

Governmental bills in the parliamentary phase

It was already mentioned that the government proposes on average more than every other bill. Once the governmental bill is put on the agenda, its probability of success is very high, reaching on average 80 percent.[48] Thus, while the Czech government does not have the virtual monopoly on the content of the legislative agenda as in other countries with a parliamentary form of governance, its position is still prominent.[49]

Other noticeable aspect of the Czech situation is the will of deputies to amend the majority of government bills. The original form of the government bill therefore sometimes undergo significant changes, but the government has no formal opportunity to influence this (rather unfortunate) trend because the governmental bills do not enjoy protection from amending.[50] The "only" tool the government has at its disposal is its majority in the Chamber of Deputies and this is susceptible to failure, mainly if the majority is low (usual situation) or the deputies unify against the government. The only alternative instrument available to prevent unwanted changes to the original version of the bill is its withdrawal from the legislative process in the Chamber of Deputies.[51] This situation shows that while the government shall normatively operate as a dominant legislative actor, it lacks wider competences in the later stages of the legislative process.

This statement is also confirmed by the government's role in the process of deliberation of non-governmental bills in the Chamber of Deputies. Although the government has (according to Art. 44 of the Constitution) a right to express its view on non-governmental proposals of bills (which can also be understood as the right of other participants in the legislative

---

48 The success rate oscillated from 72.5 percent in 1996-2002 election period to 86 percent in 2002-2006 election period, see Kolář. et al. 2013, *ibid*, p. 444. In 2013-2017 election period the success rate reached 80 percent (301 out of 376), recent data extracted from the Chamber of Deputies website http://public.psp.cz/en /sqw/sntisk.sqw.

49 See Kysela and Kokeš 2018, *ibid*, p. XC.

50 See J Kysela, 'Moc výkonná jako činitel právotvorby. Přehled rolí a problémů' (2018) 51 Správní právo (Legislativní příloha) II–XXIII.

51 For example, during the 2013-2017 term, the government withdrew 14 proposed bills.

process to know the government's opinion),[52] its opinion has only recommendatory character. There have been numerous cases of circumvention of the governmental initiative through submitting even comprehensive bills mainly by single or group of deputies; the Constitutional Court commented on the practice and called it "disguised legislative initiative" of the government.[53]

Conclusion

This chapter analyzed the legislative process especially within the executive (the government) in the Czech Republic, its legal (formal) framework and emphasized some specific features linked to practical functioning of the government coalition. Many aspects of these specific features cause that the legislative process suffers from numerous deficiencies, resulting in the current rather problematic state of law-making and low quality of legal order in general in the Czech Republic. The contribution focused on selected features within the preparatory phase of legislative process, i.e. initiation and drafting stage where a dominant role is played by the government and/or ministries (and its legislative departments as the drafters). Unfortunately, there are no easy ways out from these problems. Preparation and adoption of more precise legal framework of preparatory phase of legislative process could be one of them, but certainly not sufficient without changing the attitude of the executive to law-making as such. For example, ex post evaluation of a necessity to propose new legal regulation could significantly help but only if the notion that a "new law is always the best answer to everything" is breached. Nevertheless, it is clear that a first step to solve any problems is to analyze them. Hopefully, this book will contribute to this goal.

---

52 If the bill concerned is non-governmental, the Chairperson of the Chamber of Deputies sends it to the government and asks it to express its view on the bill within 30 days of the receipt. The position paper (so called "white paper") of the government is sent to deputies and political groups.

53 Judgment no. Pl. US 77/06. See also J Kysela, 'Tvorba práva v ČR: truchlohra se šťastným koncem?' (2006) 7 Právní zpravodaj 8-11.

Germany

Ulrich Karpen

Introduction

The question seems to be simple: who is responsible for drafting the version of a law which then is introduced into parliament for deliberation and adoption? The answer is somewhat more complicated, because actors and procedures before and after the initiative are to a large extent imprinted by the *principles of the democratic rule-of-law-state,* which is the constitutional frame of Central European countries and, by the way, the main content of the Copenhagen criteria of the European Union member states. To another extent law-production in each country is regulated by its national constitution. A well-known aphorism of the psychiatrist Scott Peck suggests, "that we should share our similarities and celebrate our differences."[1] If we understand why and how in applying common standards, others legislate differently than how we do, we are encouraged to compare and learn, and to improve our methods or retain our own legislative style.

How large is the body of laws which is produced by the German legislator? The Federal Diet (*Bundestag*) in its 18th session (2013-2017) adopted 548 laws, which makes 130 per year. In the 19th session (since 2017) until now the number is 112.[2] The majority of these laws are amendments to other laws. During the same 18th session government released 1300 statutory instruments (ordinances), as authorized in detail by statutory law.[3] That makes 350 instruments per year. Both laws and ordinances are published in the Official Federal Gazette. The volume of the 18th session Gazette is some 12.000 pages. These figures are not untypical for the workload of the parliament. 60 to 70 percent of laws and statutory instru-

---

1 *W Voermans*, 'Styles of Legislation and Their effects' (2011) 32 Statute Law Review 38.
2 Deutscher Bundestag, Parlamentsdokumentation, Statistik der Gesetzgebung, 18. und 19. Wahlperiode.
3 Deutscher Bundestag, Parlamentsdokumentation, Statistik der Gesetzgebung – Überblick 18. Wahlperiode.

ments are caused, or determined, by EU-law,[4] namely in the fields of medicine and drugs, environment, agriculture and food regulation. EU-law does not leave too much room today for member states' legislation. One has to take into account that in Germany, as a Federation, next to the Federal parliament 16 *Länder* parliaments are legislating in their areas of authority, namely communal responsibilities, education, science, police and infrastructure.

To understand who is responsible for drafting and initiating bills, again, one needs to start from the general understanding that laws are planned, drafted, adopted, implemented, and (if necessary) amended in a multistep procedure, in which all constitutional organs participate. The main elements of the legislative cycle are:

- the impulse, the idea, to legislate on a matter or to solve a problem;
- the analysis of the problem or matter
- policy setting
- definition of targets and instruments
- drafting
- initiating into parliament
- deliberation and adoption of the draft in parliament
- signing and promulgation of the law
- implementation
- monitoring of the implementation
- amendments (if necessary) and starting a new cycle.[5]

This paper focusses on developing the content and drafting laws. Drafting, mostly, takes place in line Ministries, in the UK in the Office of Parliamentary Counsel,[6] in France often in the Sécrétariat Général du Gouvernement.[7] The initiative, introduction of the bill into the parliamentary procedure is taken by the government or – as we will see – by parliament itself.

---

4 Frankfurter Allgemeine Zeitung (FAZ) of 21 December 2017, p. 7.
5 *U Karpen,* 'Introduction' in U Karpen and H Xanthaki (eds) *Legislation in Europe, A Comprehensive Guide for Scholars and Practitioners* (Bloomsbury 2017), 1-16.
6 *SJ Bates,* 'United Kingdom' in U Karpen (ed), *Legislation in European Countries* (Nomos 1997) 431.
7 *C Bergeal, Rédiger un texte normatif* (Berger-Levrault 2012) 137.

Overview of the German constitutional and political system

The particularities of the German "cradle of laws" consequently are imprinted by the *characteristics of the German Constitution, the Basic Law of 1949*. According to the Basic Law, Germany has a parliamentary democratic system of government, it is a federation, it is a *rule-of-law-state* with a Constitutional Court controlling all state activities, namely for the purpose of protecting individual rights, and it is a *social state (Art. 20 of the Basic Law)*.

It is a parliamentary government-state insofar as the majority of bills (74 percent) originate from the government. Only rarely is the drafting of complicated bills outsourced to law firms (which is a very controversial matter!). Bills may also originate from the floor of the Federal Diet (15 percent).[8]

Germany is a federation, put together by 16 states. The *Länder* participate in federal legislation in the Federal Council (*Bundesrat*). It consists of members of the *Länder* governments. Each *Land* has – based on its population – 3-6 votes; all together the Federal Council has 68 votes. Only in a very broad understanding of the term the Federal Council may be looked at as a second chamber of parliament. 11 percent of the initiatives for federal legislation originate from the Federal Council. These bills are drafted in ministries or cabinet offices of one *Land* or joint *Länder*.

Germany is a *rule-of-law-state* with a strong Constitutional Court. The Federal Constitutional Court is the "watchdog" of legislation and it is the *epicentre of Germany's democracy*. It has a breath-taking mandate both in scope and depth. It is one of the world's most important constitutional tribunals that operates as a "quasi-legislative institution". If the Court declares a law as enacted to be unconstitutional, parliament has to amend and redraft the law, partly with detailed specifications given by the Court in content and wording. It is therefore fair to say that the Court is a "midwife at the cradle of law". If the Federal Constitutional Court[9] – on individual complaints of unconstitutionality of law – finds that the body of law is defective and fragmentary, it may – and did so – set a deadline for

---

8 Deutscher Bundestag, Parlamentsdokumentation, Statistik der Gesetzgebung, 18. und 19. Wahlperiode.

9 *U Karpen*, 'Efficacy, Effectiveness, Efficiency' in K Meßerschmidt and AD Oliver-Lalana (eds), *Rational Lawmaking under Review, Legisprudence According to the German Federal Constitutional Court* (Springer 2016) 309.

enacting a law with specified content; here the Court seems to be a "replacement legislator".

Finally, Germany is a *social state*. Since the Basic Law widely, at least by the Federal Constitutional Court, is looked at as a value codex, imprinted by the human rights catalogue with human dignity at the top, the Federal Constitutional Court may order particular social, including financial, facts to be established by the legislator, e.g. a monetary existence minimum to be paid by the state to each asylum seeker.

The basic framework of the legislative process

To respond to the question of who is responsible for initiating, drafting, deliberating a bill until it is processed and adopted in parliament, one should mention the following important points.

The *impulse* to make a law – and not to leave the regulation to the lower levels of delegated legislation or administration regulations – originates in coalition agreements, general guidelines or leadership decisions of the Federal Chancellor as Head of government, decision of a minister within his scope of responsibility, pressure by the media ("It's a scandal! The legislator has to act!") or motions in parliament nudged by individuals or groups of deputies.

The *draft* is then introduced in the Federal Diet by the government through the Federal Council, which may comment on the bill within six weeks. Or it is introduced by the Federal Council via the government, which may comment within six weeks (Art. 76 of the Basic Law). After having been adopted by the Federal Diet, the draft goes to the Federal Council. If both houses disagree, the draft may be negotiated by a *Joint Committee*. If a bill, according to the Basic Law, requires the consent of the Second House, the Federal Council may adopt or reject the bill. If the latter happens, the bill is dead. If the bill, as passed by the Federal Diet, does not require the consent of the Second House, the Second House may object the bill. This objection may be overruled by the Federal Diet (Art. 76 of the Basic Law).

Finally, a bill may be initiated from the floor of the Federal Diet, be it by a parliamentary group or 5 percent of the members not organised in a faction (35 members out of 750 members of the House). This bill would then be processed by the government, Federal Diet and Federal Council, as described before (Art. 76 of the Basic Law).

All in all, after the political impulse three organs are participating in drafting and deliberating a bill: both houses of parliament and the government. The Federal Constitutional Court may have the last say, though. So in the three-powers-structure of the separation-of-powers-rule-of-law-state all three are, to a certain extent, "midwifes at the cradle of law".

The practice of drafting and negotiating governmental bills in Germany

The main competence and responsibility for drafting a bill lies with the lead ministry. The minister as a member of cabinet is, of course, a politician. The members of the departmental units and subunits, who in fact do the drafting work, are civil servants and, as such, stand "in a relationship of service and loyalty defined by public law".[10] The traditional principles of the professional civil service (Art. 33 of the Basic Law) require a nonpartisan execution of their function. The line ministry[11] has to inform the Chancellor of the preparation of a bill, has to develop the draft until it is "fit for submission to the cabinet's decision", is in charge of the ex-post control of the adopted law, and – if necessary – the first step of amendment, if required by impact assessment. Very often, the responsibilities of ministries are overlapping, e.g. freeway tolls: the Ministries of Traffic and Environment; security legislation and asylum seekers: the Ministry of the Interior and the Foreign Office. Mostly, the Minister of Finance is involved. If there are differences of opinion between the main ministries involved, extensive or expansive preparations should be started or instigated before the cabinet has taken a decision. The responsible ministries have to submit a consented bill to the cabinet.[12] In drafting and negotiating a new bill, the ministry officials have to apply the governmental "Guidelines for Drafting Legal provisions and Administrative Regulations".[13]

Furthermore, there are different bodies and institutions which have to participate in the drafting process. The most important one is the *National*

---

10 *U Karpen*, 'Civil Service in Germany' (2019) 29 European Review of Public Law 1.
11 Details are regulated on in the Rules of Procedure of the Federal Government, 11 May 1951 (joint Ministerialblatt of the Federal Government, 137, as of 22 October 2002 (Gaz 848).
12 Ibid.
13 *Bundesministerium des Inneren, Handbuch zur Vorbereitung von Rechts- und Verwaltungsvorschriften* (Berlin 2012).

Regulatory Control Council.[14] This Council was established in 2006 at the Federal Chancellery. It is only bound by the mandate conferred by the establishing Act and is independent in its work. It examines the compliance costs for new regulations for citizens, the business sector, and public administration, especially for small and medium-sized enterprises. It applies the Standard Cost Model, the review shall not cover the intended purposes and aims of regulations. The Control Council examines all draft regulations of Federal Ministries before submission to the cabinet. In the same manner it controls the drafts initiated by the Federal Council and drafts from the floor of the Federal Diet when requested. The Council is also available to act in an advisory capacity to the leading and co-advisory standing committee of the two houses of parliament.[15]

The Council is a member of *RegWatch Europe*.[16] This is the banner under which Europe's seven independent national advisory boards coordinate to address and maximise the benefits of Europe's smart regulations agenda and regulatory burdens. It combines the strengths of the Dutch, German, Norwegian, Czech, English, Swedish, and Finnish control councils. Since 2016 the Regulatory Scrutiny Board of the EU does the same work,[17] following the High Level Group of Independent Stakeholders on Administrative Burdens (Stoiber Commission).

Before the ministerial draft is submitted to the Cabinet for adoption, it must be sent to the *Federal Ministry of Justice* to be examined in accordance with systematic and legal scrutiny. The Ministry, applying the "Manual for Drafting Legislation"[18] has to determine whether legal provisions are compatible with the Basic Law and other pieces of law. Accord-

---

14 Act on the Establishment of a National Regulatory Control Council of 14 August 2006, as amended on 16 March 2011, FedLaw Gazette I 420.

15 For more details see *The National Regulatory Control Council (in a nutshell)* (Berlin 2016), and *10 Years National Regulatory Control Council – Annual Report – 10 years of NKR – Good Record on Cutting Red Tape* (Berlin 2016); S Naundorf, *Regulatory Impact Assessment – Examples from Germany*, OECD Workshop, Bangkok, 2 April 2019; OECD, *OECD Regulatory Compliance Cost Assessment Guide* (Paris 2016).

16 Available at http://www.actal.nl/english/regwatcheurope, Ref. Ares (2016) 5764766 – 05/10/2016.

17 Available at http://ec.europa.eu/info/files/regulatory-scrutiny-board-rules-procedur e_en.

18 Federal Ministry of Justice (ed), *Manual for Drafting Legislation* (Berlin 2008); in German: *Handbuch der Rechtsförmlichkeit, Empfehlungen zur Gestaltung von Gesetzen und Rechtsverordnungen* (Köln 2008).

ing to the "Joint Rules of Procedure of the Federal Ministries" the Ministry of Justice also checks whether the bill is in conformity with European law.

The next step before the involvement of Cabinet is the examination of the bill by the *Federal Commissioner for Effectiveness in Public Administration* which has a special mandate by the Head of the Federal Office of Statistics. The language used in bills must be correct and understandable to everyone as far as possible. In general, bills must be submitted to the *Unit for Legal Drafting Support* to review their linguistic accuracy and comprehensivity. Bills should be submitted in as early a stage as possible. The reviewers are civil servants in the Ministry of Justice.

It goes without saying that an *exchange of opinions and views on the bill with all other ministries* is a primordial requirement of the procedure. Participation of the following institutions must be made sure as soon as possible:

- the governments of the *Länder*
- associations of cities and other local authorities
- the expert community
- groups of interest
- stakeholders
- affected persons and groups
- members of parliament (who may demand to receive the text early).

The line ministry shall collect information and advice from all sources, which are knowledgeable and available. If an *oral hearing* is conducted by the lead ministry with regard to the bill, all participants, as mentioned, are allowed to submit opinions and speak out. If it is intended to make bills available to the *press* or other bodies officially not involved, the ministry – or the Chancellor – decides on the appropriate ways to do it. The government finally initiates the bill (Art. 76 of the Basic Law) – in a cabinet conference – to the Federal Diet.

The fate of governmental bills in the parliament

Parliament discusses bills in leading and co-advisory standing committees, which may have joint sessions. The Federal Diet adds expertise to the bill, be it by parliamentary questions of parliamentary groups or individual members of parliament to government.[19] It may schedule hearings and – if the matter of a given bill is complex – can set up *enquètes*, e.g. of the situation of culture in the nation. Parliament may establish permanent advisory bodies, e.g. for ethics in medicine.

The *Standing Committee of Research, Technology and Technology Assessment* may ask the advice of the *Office of Technology Assessment* at the Federal Diet, which currently is outsourced to an independent *Institute of Technology Assessment and Systems Analysis* in Karlsruhe, which is linked with the *Association of Engineers* and *Association of Electronics*. The procedure is similar to that of the National Regulatory Control Council. Similar responsibilities lie with the *Parliamentary Advisory Council of Sustainable Development*. It has to make sure that life today is not at the expense of the future.

There is a second body of linguistic control of the bill next to the unit in the Ministry of Justice, but this one in parliament. It is the Editorial Committee at the Federal Diet. Finally, one has to mention the *Research Service of the parliamentary administration*. It is a section of the staff of parliament. Some 65 scholars are assigned to the standing committees of the Federal Diet. The staff members are accessible by each member of parliament.

The second initiator of bills is – next to government – the Federal Council (11 percent of bills originate there). Bills of the Federal Council shall be submitted to the Federal Diet by the Federal government within six weeks. The government shall state its own views. Since majorities in the Federal Council and in the Federal Diet usually differ in parties and coalition perspective, the two chambers of parliament add to pluralism of policy and - one must say – do aggravate the legislative process.

Bills may also originate from the floor of the Federal Diet (15 percent), be it by a parliamentary group or 5 percent of members of the House (Art. 76 of the Basic Law). The bills are sent to government, then to the Federal Diet, and the Federal Council. Some of these bills are "pocket bills" in that the texts are written by officials in the competent ministries.

The Basic Law definitely prefers the *representative democracy*. Direct legislation by the people is provided for only in one case: the new delimitation of the federal territory. Although the drawing of new borders of

---

19 *U Karpen, 'Regulatory Impact Assessment (RIA)*: Current Situation and Prospects in the German Parliament' (2015) 101 Amicus Curiae 14.

Länder – namely mergers – seems to be required and even necessary, no such initiative was successful until now. In fact, some very small *Länder* can fulfil their tasks only with significant financial assistance of the other *Länder*.

In the *Länder* and their constitutions, direct legislation of the people is quite common. Different forms of initiatives, petitions, and referenda present a colourful picture. Since "more participation" is a vivid topic in political discussion, one can observe a "race of *Länder* to direct democratic procedures". Of course, everywhere the same problems arise: small majorities which decide; budget-decisions and a sort of "ping-pong" game between initiatives and *Länder* parliaments.

As has been mentioned, the Basic Law, by the strength of the Federal Constitutional Court, is virtually identical with the Court's Interpretation. As the Chief Justice of the US Supreme Court, Charles Evans Hughes said in 1907: "We are bound by the Constitution, but the Constitution is what the judges say it is."[20] The Federal Constitutional Court does not only control the constitutionality of the legislative process in a formal sense, but in a substantive sense as well. It judges whether democratic elements of the procedure (e.g. publicity, transparency, and participation) have been observed, whether rule-of-law principles have been kept (e.g. due process, practicability, and fairness), and, finally, whether basic elements of the value system reflected in the Basic Law have been taken into account by the legislator (e.g. proportionality, solidarity, subsidiarity).

Conclusion

Who is responsible for the drafting and the negotiation of bills in Germany? There are many mothers and fathers standing by the "cradle of bills", nursing and assisting, many institutions, bodies, and persons. No bill, wherever drafted in this complicated system, leaves parliament as it has been planned beforehand. The machinery has been invented to create a

---

20 Speech before the Chamber of Commerce, Elmira/NY on 3 May 1907, published in C Evans, *Addresses and Papers of Charles Evans Hughes, Governor of NY, 1906-1908* (Wentworth Press 2016) 139.

democratic, just, effective, and – all in all – *rational* product: the law.[21] But we should always be aware of our limitations. Legislation should be as good, as precise, as efficient, and as rational as possible, but it will never be mathematics. As John Dickinson said on 13 August 1787 in the Constitutional Assembly of the United States of America in Philadelphia: "The life of the law has not been logic: it has been experience."[22]

---

21 Examples in *U Karpen, I Breutz and A Nünke, Die Gesetzgebung der Großen Koalition in der ersten Hälfte der Legislaturperiode des 16. Deutschen Bundestages (2005-2007)* (FHM Verlag 2008).

22 Century of Law Making for a New Nation: US Congressional Documents and Debates, 1774-1875, (1991) 2 Farrand's Records 278.

Hungary

Zsolt Szabó[1]

Introduction

Since the fall of the socialist regime in 1989/90, Hungary is a functioning parliamentary democracy: a republic with a multiparty political system, governed by the rule of law. Like the constitutional and institutional framework of governance, also the system of legislation underwent major changes compared to the one-party-system at the end of the 1980s, when by-laws and other low-level sources of law determined significant policy issues, restricted fundamental rights; transparency and democratic legitimation were lacking. Nowadays one can witness the opposite: high-level legislative acts (laws requiring either simple or qualified majority) dominate the legislative scene, turning parliament into a legislative machinery, leaving no time for thorough preparation and deliberation, adopting laws overloaded with details which would sometimes better fit into secondary legislation.

As a result, legislation rules mainly focus on procedures and formalities, while policy contents and quality gain less attention, and impact assessments aren't taken into serious consideration.[2] Especially – but not exclusively - the FIDESZ-government in office since 2010 has come up with an ambitious legislative agenda, including many accelerated procedures and frequently modified legislation – and some corrective procedural measures (e.g. limiting the number of fast track procedures) after 2014.[3]

---

1 This study was also supported by the János Bolyai Research Scholarship of the Hungarian Academy of Sciences.
2 R Franczel, 'Kormányzati döntéshozatal 2010-2014 között' (2015) Kodifikáció és Közigazgatás 6.
3 For a general overview of this period see G Ilonszki, 'From minimum to subordinate: A final Verdict? The Hungarian parliament, 1990–2010' (2011) 13 Journal of Legislative Studies 38–58; G Ilonszki and K Jager, 'Hungary: Changing government advantages – Challenging a dominant executive' in E Rasch and G Tsebelis (eds), *Role of the governments in legislative agenda-setting* (Routledge 2011) 95–110.

This paper describes the current institutional-legislative framework and practice of preparation of statutory legislation in Hungary. After introducing the institutions, procedures and some data related to legislation, internal workflows of the government and the role of the relevant actors will be analysed.

Overview of the constitutional and political system

The form of government in Hungary – as well as political practice - is parliamentarian. The main organ of state power in Hungary is the unicameral legislature (*Országgyűlés*) with 199 members (MPs), elected for four years by direct universal suffrage. The Cabinet (*Kormány*) is politically strongly linked to parliament, according to the principles of parliamentary governance. The head of the state, the president (*Köztársasági elnök*) is a representative position, without effective control rights towards parliament, elected by the legislature. His main role is to safeguard the proper functioning the three main branches of power and promulgate laws adopted by parliament. The president also has the right to introduce legislation in parliament. However, presidents hardly ever made any use of this right, apart from few legislative proposals at the beginning of the 1990s. More frequent is the suspensive veto of the president: he may return any adopted statue for reconsideration to parliament, but has to sign them nevertheless, if parliament adopts it again with or without amendments. The main form of state power in Hungary is representative democracy, the institution of direct democracy (referendum) is used only very exceptionally. The state structure and fundamental rights are set out in the Fundamental Law (*Alaptörvény*), the country's written constitution, dating back to 2011.

The operative executive organ of the country, the Cabinet, has among others the task to take the necessary measures to ensure public order and security, to prepare and implement the state budget, to determine the foreign policy and conclude international agreements on its behalf. Generally, the Cabinet is also responsible for executing laws adopted by parliament.

The Cabinet consists of the Prime Minister (*Miniszterelnök*) and the Cabinet ministers. The Prime Minister is not just a formal leader of Cabinet: he also defines and directs its policy. He is elected by a simple majority vote of the MPs, while ministers are proposed by the Prime Minister, and appointed (and relieved) of their duties by the president. The Cabinet bears a collective political responsibility towards parliament. The central role of the Prime Minister is reflected by the provision that it is not possible to initiate a vote of no-confidence against an individual minister, only against the Prime Minister, who represents the whole Cabinet. In order to guarantee stability, the Fundamental Law makes only the constructive form of the confidence vote possible: the majority of MPs have to agree on the new Prime Minister before withdrawing confidence from the previous one.

The establishment of ministries falls within the competence of parliament and a law defines their name and broad portfolio in each legislative term,[4] while the detailed tasks of the ministries are set out by the Cabinet in a decree.[5] Each ministry is headed by a single responsible minister who is also a member of the Cabinet. Under ministers, state secretaries are responsible for a certain policy field.

In lack of a second chamber or other kind of co-legislator in Hungary, the main 'check and balance' to parliament's legislation is the Constitutional Court (*Alkotmánybíróság*). The Court, established in 1989, followed the model of the German Federal Constitutional Court, controls the constitutionality of legislation and judicial decisions. It comprises a separate branch of state power and is not considered to be part of the judiciary. By the end of the 1990s, the Court developed a case law which was of great importance as regards the new constitutional system, many of those principles were later enacted in the Fundamental Law in 2011.

The judiciary is independent from the legislative and executive powers, it is comprised by a separate ordinary and administrative court system. Ordinary courts are local, municipal courts, appellate courts and the Supreme Court (*Kúria*) as final instance. Courts directly interpret the acts of the legislation, while the Constitutional Court checks any legislative acts against the constitution and may strike them or parts of them down if they are in contradiction with the constitution. Replacing the annulled legislation, however, is in the exclusive competence of the parliament.

The Constitutional Court is therefore an important actor in the field of legislation, having quite a wide range of competences.[6] It has the sole right to interpret the Fundamental Law; it provides normative standards

---

4 E.g. Law no. V/2018 on the List of ministries of Hungary.
5 E.g. Government decree no. 94/2018 on the Tasks and responsibilities of the Members of the Government.
6 Besides supervision of legislation, the Constitutional Court has the opportunity to review court verdicts with regard to fundamental rights ('constitutional complaint')

and ex-ante as well as ex-post supervision over the constitutionality of legislation (an ex-ante supervision takes place after parliament adopted but the president not yet promulgated the law, an ex-post takes place after promulgation); it also reconciles collisions between international and domestic law. The Court may also determine the violation of the constitution by an omission if a legislative body omitted to adopt legislation necessary for implementing a certain constitutional provision. Also ordinary court judges may initiate the procedure if they conclude that the law they are to interpret contradicts the Fundamental Law. The Court also establishes the public responsibilities of the head of state and other public officials; and it determines the spheres of authority of municipalities and local authorities, and interprets limitations on public referendums.[7]

Legal and institutional framework for the preparation of legislation

Sources of law and their role in the legal system

As in other civil law countries, in Hungary, below the constitution, the highest sources of law are parliament-made laws. Besides statutory legislation, parliament holds constituent power as well: it may approve and amend the constitution with qualified majority (2/3 of all MPs) . The constitution may be thus seen as quite flexible: the incumbent two-third majority may amend or adopt constitution anytime without involving any other organs or calling for a referendum. As a result, the constitution has constantly been subject of changes; the current Fundamental law underwent seven amendments since its adoption in 2011.

The Fundamental Law (Art. T) describes the four levels of legislation in following hierarchy:

- the Fundamental Law,
- laws adopted by the parliament (*törvény*),
- governmental and ministerial decrees (*kormányrendelet/miniszteri rendelet*), adopted by the Cabinet as a whole or a minister (they become

---

on the initiative of the person affected by the case if they were based on unconstitutional legislation or were based on constitutional grounding but came to an unconstitutional result.

7 Law no. CVI/2011 on the Constitutional Court.

valid only if published in the Official Gazette of Hungary – *Magyar Közlöny*)
* and decrees of local governments (*önkormányzati rendelet*).

The hierarchy between these sources of law mean that a decree may not contradict a statutory law, and no legal source may contradict the Fundamental Law. The Fundamental Law also accepts the universally recognized rules and regulations of international law without any further implementation, and guarantees to harmonize domestic legal acts with the obligations assumed under international law. According to the dualist practice, parliament and Cabinet need to implement international treaties in legislation of their own domain. A significant number of all legislative acts (appr. 1/3 of all laws) are enactments of international agreements.

Laws are normally adopted by simple majority vote in parliament. However, some laws need a qualified majority approval, as specified in the Fundamental Law.[8] These are called cardinal laws (*sarkalatos törvény*). The distinction between ordinary and cardinal laws was a result of the compromise between old and new elites in 1989. The issues requiring qualified majority are thus not selected by value, weight or importance, rather by a political agreement reached at the roundtable discussions thirty years ago. Since many policy areas are affected, major reforms need a compromise between Cabinet and opposition. However, between 1994 and 1998, and multiple times since 2010, the Cabinet has a 2/3 majority in parliament and can make any changes, including amendments to the constitution. It is important to stress that in theory, there is no hierarchy in the legal system between ordinary and cardinal laws. In practice, however, cardinal laws often work as a barrier to ordinary laws' amendments if the required qualified majority in parliament is lacking.

This legislative framework implicates that laws enjoy a strong preference in the Hungarian legal system. Besides the Fundamental Law, which describes some legislative subjects to be regulated exclusively by law,[9] parliament generally may expand its almost unlimited legislative activity

---

8 Some examples: citizenship, use of national symbols, protection of families, religious organisations, operation and management of political parties, freedom of press, military service, election procedure, right of parliamentary inquiry, establishment of regulatory organs, powers, organisation and operation of the Constitutional Court, operation of the parliament, judicial system.
9 A few examples: creation of new administrative organs, rules of self-protection in criminal law, conditions by creation of religious organisations, content of freedom

to any areas previously not or only partly regulated by law. The Fundamental Law requires also that the legislation affecting fundamental rights and duties to be enacted in statutory legislation. Furthermore, parliament has the exclusive right to regulate fields which are already regulated by law. Once parliament has brought the matter within the scope of statutory regulation, this may be modified or repealed only by the adoption of another law. As a result, the number of yearly adopted laws is increasing, also because it is often a matter of prestige for the line ministries to place their legislation to the highest possible source of law. Replacing laws by lower level instruments hardly ever happens, the necessary time and political will is hardly there. The legislative competence of the Cabinet is limited to the areas not regulated by laws.

As a result of this dominance of laws, their number is relatively high in the legal system. This is in huge contrast with the situation in the past socialist regime where only a few laws were adopted by parliament each year, and legislation was generally practiced by different subjects (Presidential Council, Council of Ministers) deciding behind closed doors. After this extremity, nowadays one can witness the opposite: between 1990 and 2020 parliament adopted more than 5000 laws, more than half of the amending previously adopted ones. Parliament passes almost 200 laws each year, the number have slightly increased with time.[10] Laws are changing rapidly: only one third of the 5000 laws are currently in force, the others – mostly due to their merely amending character – have already been repealed. The current situation is shown also from the following numbers of legislative acts currently in force:

Table 1: Legislation currently in force in Hungary

Legislative act	Quantity	Average length[11]
Law	1849	121500
Government decree	2517	50700
Ministerial decree	2827	60722

Source: www.njt.hu (National Legal Database, as of March 2020).

---

of teaching, conditions of labour contracts, conditions of releasing university tuition fees, social benefits.

10 Corruption Research Centre Budapest: A magyar törvényhozás minősége 1998–2012 – leíró statisztikák, available at www.crbc.eu.

11 Number of characters, including footnotes on amendments.

Delegated legislation plays a secondary role in the Hungarian legal system, contrary to an ideal situation where primary and secondary legislation have the same importance notwithstanding the hierarchy between them. By-laws are sometimes seen as 'second-class' legislative acts, thus the general intention of the executive is to regulate as much as possible in law. The numbers of average length show also that laws are normally more detailed than secondary legislation, the opposite of an ideal situation.

It should be added that delegation in Hungary does not mean empowerment, i.e. delegation of legislative power of one legislative organ to the other, it rather means activating the legislative power of a lower legislative organ by a higher one. Parliament may never delegate its law-making power to the Cabinet, it may only require the Cabinet to legislate by adopting a decree in a subject matter within its own legislative domain. Cabinet may never adopt legislation on statutory level, not even in extraordinary circumstances. In case of delegation, the Cabinet is obliged to act, although there are normally no time limits and consequences for non-acting. However, the Cabinet may not sub-delegate legislative power it received from the parliament, as well as ministers may not sub-delegate their legislative tasks to any other organ. While Cabinet may adopt a decree on its own initiative (in case the subject is not yet regulated by law) as well as by statutory delegation, a minister may only adopt a decree upon delegation.

As seen above, instead of a pyramidal structure, where ministerial decrees would represent the majority of the legal acts with the most detailed rules, we are witnessing a 'top-heavy' structure of legislation with laws on the first place in number as well as in length. Of course, the basis of the extensive statutory legislation is the expertise of the Cabinet: the majority of laws adopted by parliament were Cabinet initiatives. The Cabinet normally spends more time and efforts with preparing bills for submission than drafting its own secondary legislation.

Legal sources on legislative drafting

Besides the Fundamental law, another important legal source of legislation is the Law on Legislation (LoL) from 2010, which sets out the general rules of law-making, including:

- the prohibition of retroactive effect (with the exception of an exclusively positive effect on all stakeholders),
- the requirements of delegated and transitional legislation,
- the general rules of geographic and personal effect of legislative acts,
- the formal rules of amending and repealing existing legislation,
- the obligation of impact assessment,
- the rules of justification (reasoning) of legislative proposals,
- the rules on promulgation, transparency and availability of the legislation.[12]

The Law also regulates the internal rules of organs of public law (*közjogi szervezetszabályozó eszköz*), which may only affect persons within the respective organ and do not have general effect. An important issue, public consultations of legislation has been outsourced in 2010 and is being governed by a separate law ever since (see details further below).[13]

Legislative drafting rules are to be found in a decree of the Minister of Justice.[14] With its 150 articles, it is the longest legislative act from the domain of legislation. Beyond the normative provisions of legislative drafting, there is an equally long set of annexes attached to it, providing textual examples for formulation of legal provisions (e.g. use of references, formula for amendments). The decree contains provisions on linguistic aspects, designs the formal structure and sections of legislative acts (book, chapter, title, article, paragraph, point) as well as the logical structure (preamble, general provisions, detailed provisions, final provisions).

Another ministerial decree that need mentioning regulates ex-ante and ex-post impact assessment of all legislative acts.[15] The brief decree (only eight articles!) contains the tasks, describes the documents and their content during the impact assessment process. An 'impact assessment form' is attached to the decree as annex, which need to be filled for all legislative proposals. However, the form is a one-page document with three chapters each with open space subject to free formulations: 'I. Budgetary impacts', 'II. Administrative burdens', 'III. Other impacts.' The previous legislation, which was in force between 2011 and 2016, foresaw a more detailed eval-

---

12 Law no. CXXX of 2010 on Legislation.
13 Law no. CXXXI/2010 on the Social participation in the preparation of legislation.
14 Decree no. 61/2009 of the Minister of Justice and law enforcement on legislative drafting.
15 Decree no. 12/2016 of the Minister leading the Prime Minister's office on Ex-ante and ex-post impact assessment.

uation form, which was albeit not used in regular practice and was radically simplified in 2016.

The practice of impact assessments corresponds to the weak regulatory framework: as a pre-2010 comparative research found, Hungary almost altogether ignored the preparation of regulatory impact assessments. Few regulatory issues were addressed, and if they were, they were introduced in an ad hoc manner. Even if Hungary was the first in the region to introduce RIAs in legislative procedure, the practice showed a fragmented, sporadic and formal attitude towards them.[16] Since 2010 the RIA procedure has been streamlined and used in a more systematic way, but it is rather a tool to control the administrative services than to secure quality legislation.[17] The LoL only foresees impact assessment of governmental bills, proposals from the MPs are excluded.

Even from the structure of legal sources dealing with legislation it is obvious that the formal rules dominate and policy content quality tools are of secondary importance. Elaborate, detailed, sometimes rigorous provisions govern the formalities, while the content and quality of legislation lag behind.

Analysis of practical functioning of the preparatory process

There are four possible proposers of statutory legislation in Hungary, as set out in the Fundamental Law: the Cabinet, MPs (either as single proposers or as groups of MPS), the President of Hungary, and parliamentary committees. In practice, the latter two hardly practice their right. On the contrary, many MPs, especially opposition MPs submit legislative proposals to parliament, even if these are hardly ever approved, and often do not even enter into parliamentary procedure, not being discussed either by committee or by plenary. There is no procedural guarantee of debating opposition bills, even a minimum of them. Most laws adopted by parliament start their career as Cabinet proposals.

By Cabinet proposals, the procedure of preparation of bills begins with the submission of the legislative plan on a sessional basis, as the Law on

---

16 K Staroňová, 'Regulatory Impact Assessment: Formal Institutionalization and Practice' (2010) 1 Journal of Public Policy 117–136.

17 G Gajduschek, 'Előkészítetlenség és utólagos hatásvizsgálat hiánya' in J Szerk and G Gajduschek (eds), *A magyar jogrendszer állapota* (MTA TK 2016) 801.

the National Assembly requires.[18] In practice, at the beginning of each parliamentary session (semester), the Cabinet submits its legislation plan to parliament, including those bills planned to be submitted to parliament. This list is put together from the scheduled legislative proposals of the line ministries and finalized by the Prime Minister's administration. Since it happens regularly that many items from the list are not submitted or at the same time other bills appear without being originally scheduled, the plan is not treated in practice as a strategic tool of targeted government policy, rather as an information on what workload parliament has to face in the upcoming months.

The legislative plan in practice has an Excel-sheet format with columns for the name of the proposal, the responsible ministry, a short description of content in 3-4 lines, the planned month of submission to parliament, the expected month of adoption by parliament, and the volume described by one of three simple variables ('short', 'medium', 'long'). There is no textual explanation and analysis related to government policies. The plan only contains prospective laws, but not governmental or ministerial decrees.

In practice, the plan is regularly and timely submitted, but it is hardly ever fully implemented: about half of the items are dropped, and a similar number of new proposal are submitted spontaneously in the course of the legislative term.[19] If there is a shortage of time at (for example at the end of the legislative session), the political agenda normally prevails over policy planning. In autumn 2017 for example, there were 46 items on the legislative plan, in spring 2018 only one (due to the upcoming elections), for autumn 2018 there were 39 items foreseen.

As far as the intra-institutional organization is concerned, each ministry has a legal department also responsible for legislative drafting. This department is normally supervised by the administrative state secretary, the de facto director of the ministry. The details of the procedure of Cabinet's legislative preparation are set out in a decision of the Cabinet on its rules of procedure (RoPC).[20] As a first practical step of the legislative drafting procedure, this service drafts a legislative proposal, which is subject to re-

---

18 Law no. XXXVI/2012 on the National Assembly.
19 Gajduschek 2016, *ibid.*
20 Government decision no. 1044/2010 on the Rules of Procedure of the Government.

vision and approval by the minister or his cabinet.[21] This involves the 'political line' already at the very first stage of the process. It is also common that the policy departments of the ministry take part in the drafting as well, but the general responsibility lies at the legal unit. At major legislative tasks, the drafting is sometimes outsourced to a drafting committee consisting of senior experts of the particular field (eg. Civil Code, Penal Code reforms from 2012).

This 'ministerial draft' is then sent to the central coordinative unit of the Cabinet (§ 15 RoPC). This unit was traditionally placed at the Prime Minister's Office (PMO), which is a central government organ, headed, like a ministry, by a Cabinet minister. Since June 2018 however, policy legislative coordination is a responsibility of the Government Office of the Prime Minister (GOPM), a central government office, separated from the PMO, and headed by the Prime Minister himself. The coordination of Cabinet legislation is managed by the administrative state secretary of the GOPM directly supervised by the Prime Minister directly. This means that under current setup, PMO is rather a strategic coordination body than a legislative one, responsible for mainly long-term policy planning. The coordination of legislation within the Cabinet is done by the GOPM.[22] The administrative state secretary of GOPM checks whether the legislative proposal is 'in line with the general policy of the government', as the rules of procedure of the Cabinet require. High profile political issues are therefore possible to be taken into account already at this stage, even before inter-ministerial or public consultations.

After the legislative proposal (which is a detailed, paragraphed text already at this stage, and not a conceptual paper) is checked by the GOPM and the Ministry of Finance, the bill is circulated within all line ministries, and in the same time published on the website of the government for public consultation. Both lime ministries and the general public, working parallelly, have very short deadlines. The responsible ministry has the task of evaluating the consultations, finalizing the draft, and preparing it for adoption by the Cabinet (§ 12 RoPC). During inter-ministerial consultations, in almost all cases only legislative units of other ministries take part in the

---

21 For a more detailed description of the preparatory phase see some earlier works as E.g. S Pesti, 'Közpolitikai döntéshozatal Magyarországon' in G Gajduschek and T Rossiter (eds), *A közpolitika formálásának gyakorlata a brit és a magyar közigazgatásban* (Magyar Közigazgatási Intézet 2002).
22 In Hungary, the Cabinet does not have a secretary general or equivalent position.

process, policy departments very often do not have the possibility (and time) to interact. Comments of other ministries made to a legislative proposal are usually done by e-mail exchanges, and are neither open for the public nor kept in a searchable database, their content is therefore not available for further analysis.

During inter-ministerial consultations, the Ministry of Justice (MoJ) has the task to review constitutional and legal aspects, including EU-related legal matters. Therefore, all bills and draft decrees (including ministerial ones) are subject to an opinion of the MoJ during the inter-ministerial consultation, which is to be prepared in extremely short deadlines, often in one or two days, or just a few hours.[23] As a legislative expert body, MoJ sometimes interferes with the central legislative coordination body of the government (currently the GOPM). Practically, the MoJ is rather one of the line ministries, representing the legal profession, than a strategic or co-ordinative body, as it was until the mid-1990s.[24]

The process of drafting and consulting bills of the Cabinet may take several months, partly depending on the length of the proposal, but more often on the sensitivity of the area to be regulated. However no procedural rules apply to bills submitted by the MPs, except for an simple obligation to provide a reasoning for the bill (§ 18 LoL). MPs usually do not have professional drafters in their team to prepare correctly worded legislative proposals and there is only a limited staff available within the team of parliamentary groups. Also, there is neither obligation nor tradition for MPs to consult the public during drafting legislation, with the justification that MPs proposals usually address questions that have high relevance in daily politics followed by an intensive press coverage, therefore the opinion of the public is 'well known'.

While most MPs´ proposals of legislation come from the opposition[25], MPs on the Cabinet side also submit bills regularly. Typical proposals

---

23 S Pesti and R Anikó-Franczel, 'A kormány működési és szervezeti rendje (1990–2014)' in A Körösényi (ed), *A magyar politikai rendszer – negyedszázad után* (Osiris 2015) 109-134.

24 For a detailed description of the role of the Ministry of Justice see LP Salgó, *Az Igazságügyi Minisztérium szerepe a kormányzati jogszabály-előkészítésben* (Fontes Iuris 2017).

25 Legislative proposals submitted by the opposition almost never become laws. For a detailed analysis see C Nikolenyi and C Friedberg, 'Vehicles of opposition influence or agents of the governing majority? Legislative committees and private members' bills in the Hungarian *Országgyűlés* and the Israeli *Knesset* (2019) 25

made by MPs supporting the government are short provisions or amendments in bills that address a simple but politically sensitive issue. The main driver behind these type of bills is the faster procedure than the usual preparation within the government services.[26] Especially the Cabinet after the elections in 2010 used this type of fast tracking. Between 2010 and 2014, almost half of adopted laws started as MPs' bills.

The 'Law on public consultations in the preparatory phase of the legislative procedure' (LPC), adopted in 2010 contains mostly broad principles and just few details. The 'widest possible range' of public opinions (preamble) should be facilitated, allowing 'appropriate time' (§ 10) with 'the most transparency' (§ 2) during public consultations of legislative concepts or drafts. However, there are no exact numbers and data explaining these broad terms. As a general rule, only governmental bills are subject to a public consultations (§ 1). Nevertheless, many exceptions apply: bills adopted during urgent legislative procedures shall not be consulted as well as if there is danger to Hungary's important military, state security, financial, foreign policy, environmental or cultural heritage interests (§ 10).

According to the LPC, there are two forms of consultations: open consultations online, and direct consultations upon invitation on the responsible minister (§ 7). In case of an open consultation, the legislative proposal is published at the Cabinet's website. Anyone can send a comment per e-mail, but there is no administrative obligation to reply, only the receipt of the comment should be confirmed. The deadline for posting comments is the same as for inter-ministerial consultation: the general public has the same, rather limited time as the professional staff of the ministries, which makes public consultations rather unrealistic. Deadlines hardly exceed a week, and the five days set as a minimum by the rules of procedure is not respected in practice, usually the consultation only takes two or three days. The website used for consultation is embedded in the website of the Cabinet and there is no transparent, searchable database of items under public consultation.[27] The comments are also not published on the website, the

---

The Journal of Legislative Studies 358-374; R Zubek, 'Negative Agenda Control and Executive–Legislative Relations in East Central Europe, 1997–2008' (2011) 17 The Journal of Legislative Studies 172-192.
26 Gajduschek 2016, *ibid*, p. 802.
27 Database is available at http://www.kormany.hu/hu/dok#!DocumentBrowse.

ministry only has obligation to prepare a summary document with the list of those who commented and justification for rejected comments.

The other form, the 'direct consultations' are not open for the public at all. This process is based on long-term partnership agreements (covering maximum the parliamentary term) between the ministry and related stakeholders "representing wide social interest or performing scientific activity". The LPC provides a list of possible partners, including civil organizations, churches, scientific organizations, representation of nationalities, universities or chambers. There are several laws requiring consultation on certain policy issues. Subject, timeframe of consultations and the form of communication (personal negotiations are possible here, contrary to open consultations) should be set out in the agreement, which should be "made available for anyone". The strategic partners having entered into such agreements have the obligation to "represent the opinion of other organizations not having such an agreement".

In theory, it is possible to consult the legislative concept as well as the final legislative draft (§ 5). In practice, a legislative concept hardly ever exist,[28] normative texts are drafted immediately, at the very early stage of the legislative procedure. In the past decades, several stakeholders attempted to claim the negligence of public consultations at the Constitutional Court, but the Court in its consistent practice rejected these arguments, stating that the lack of consultation lies in the political responsibility of the Cabinet, and it does not affect the legal effect of the legislative acts.[29] The Court also stated that from the legal perspective, the legislative procedure as such starts in parliament, which is a forum for democratic deliberation, and the preparatory phase should be left to the proponent's (Cabinet or individual MP) discretion. The preparatory phase is therefore completely excluded from constitutional review.

The Cabinet is obliged to prepare a preliminary impact assessment with the aim to check if the proposal contains serious contradiction with existing domestic or EU law as well, and the effect of the proposal on the national budget is also assessed. The proposal is therefore accompanied by a brief preliminary legal and economic impact assessment. In practice, this assessment is only of formal nature, and is hardly taken very seriously by

---

28 T Drinóczi, *Minőségi jogalkotás és adminisztratív terhek csökkentése Európában* (HVG-ORAC 2010).

29 See for example following decisions of the Constitutional Court: 7/2004 (III. 24.), 29/2006 (VI. 21.), 87/2008 (VI. 18.), 109/2008 (IX. 26.).

any actor in the process, it has low impact on the planning or decision-making on the political level. Impact assessment sheets are being filled out, but the information is often incomplete, very general, and usually aims at a political message rather than evaluating the factual impacts.[30] This situation might be explained also by the observation that Hungarian legislative thinking is dominated by formality, overshadowing the real aims and possible impacts of legislation.[31] Legislation often becomes the target itself, instead of a tool to reach policy targets.[32]

After the inter-ministerial consultation, the proposal will be put on the agenda of the weekly meeting of administrative state secretaries of all ministries (MASS), chaired by the administrative secretary of GOPM (§ 39-50 RoPC). This format is the general preparatory forum of the Cabinet's weekly sittings where all bills and draft decrees have to pass. This is the last chance to reconcile line ministries' interests and harmonize within the government services. The meetings of MASS are not open for the public. In practice, there were estimates that in the late 1990s about one-third of agenda items were not passed and sent back to the ministries for reconsideration.[33] Since 2010, due to a more streamlined mechanism, this number is much smaller.

After the proposal is approved at MASS, it can be discussed by the Cabinet or one of its smaller circles (thematic and strategic cabinets). There are currently four such formats, headed by the responsible minister and consisting of the relevant ministers: the Cabinet for Strategic and Family issues, the Economic Cabinet, the State Security Cabinet, and the Cabinet for National Policy (§ 1 RoPC). This is another stage when politi-

---

30 A Gyűrű, 'A jogszabályok és a stratégiai tervek környezeti hatásvizsgálatának gyakorlata' (2012) Pro Futuro 85-102.

31 K Jugovits, 'A jogalkotás tartalmi megalapozottsága a jogi oktatás tükrében' (2016) Pro Publico Bono – Magyar Közigazgatás 36–49.

32 This becomes obvious as we look at the difference between level of development at legislative drafting techniques and impact assessment methodology. The latter is lagging behind the first: National Assembly services recently elaborated a software (PARLEX, available at http://www.parlament.hu/parlex) for legislative drafting and workflow which will soon be used by all governmental drafting services, including inter-ministerial consultations (the system will accordingly be extended to a network called GOVLEX). The tool makes possible to reach a high level of perfection at formal rules of drafting (numbering, references, wording etc.), while policy content and impact assessment are hardly addressed in current workflow.

33 Pesti 2002, *ibid.*

cal actors can intervene and send the issue back to an earlier stage for re-consideration. In practice, the frequency of returns highly depends on the persons involved at this decision-making stage.

Since 2010, political lines have not divided the Cabinet as there has been no coalition government in Hungary. Until 2009, various models of policy coordination between coalition parties were used. Between 1990-1994 each ministry headed by a minister from one coalition partner had a state secretary from the other (cohabitation model). During the 1994-1998 period there was a system of linked ministries attached to one single coalition party, accompanied with a strong coordination mechanism orchestrated by a steering committee and mutual veto rights. In the next period (1998-2002), the isolation (and mutual distrust) between ministries headed by different parties of the coalition became complete, and „pet projects" of ministers (whether reasonable or not) were implemented without significant coordinative control.[34] In 2009, the ruling coalition broke up, paving the way for the opposition. FIDESZ (in alliance with KDNP) won the elections in 2010, but as these parties formed common candidate lists, the Cabinet was based on a party alliance rather than coalition. The negative reputation of coalition governance has resulted in a rejection of coalitions and the popularity of the single-party governments within the general public in Hungary.

Cabinet bills in the parliamentary phase

Like in most European countries, the last decades were characterized by the emerging importance of the Cabinet and the decreasing role of the parliament in Hungary. As a result of this tendency, we can almost say that parliament does not 'legislate' any more, it is rather approving, 'rubber-stamping' legislation prepared by the Cabinet. Parliament does not have the capacity (time, expertise) to thoroughly discuss and revise the legislative drafts, it mostly gives the forum only for highlighting issues which are politically sensitive or strategically important for the parties. This tendency is strengthened by the "political government" approach of the last years, since 2010 parliament plays a decreasing role in the policy process. As following the traditional model of the 'working parliament', the Hun-

---

34 Pesti 2015, *ibid.*

garian National Assembly dedicates most if its time to formal legislation procedures, however, this time is also quite limited, thorough debates on legislative agenda items are hardly influencing the outcome.

Governmental bills, after having been approved by the Cabinet, are sent by the Prime Minister to parliament and consequently, immediately published on the parliament's website (this applies also to MPs' bills). This is the initial phase of the most transparent part of the legislative procedure: all parliamentary documents are openly accessible via the parliament's website. Having avoided the quality review of the MoJ, there is one 'checkpoint' for MPs' proposals during the parliamentary phase as these bills are subject to an additional admissibility check by a designated committee. In practice this is rather a political filter instead of a legal assessment: opposition proposals regularly fail, bills from governmental MPs normally pass. The Cabinet also needs to give its opinion on all bills submitted by MPs.

The parliamentary stage of the legislative process is regulated by the rules of procedure of the parliament[35] and the Law on the National Assembly[36]. The parliamentary debate may only start if at least six days pass after the submission of the bill.. The first main step is then the general debate (first reading) at the plenary, followed by the detailed debate in a sectoral committee (the second reading). MPs may submit amendments before the committee session, which are approved or rejected by the committee. After the committee stage, all bills are checked by the Committee for Legislation (established in 2014) as well, which may also amend the proposal. Finally, the closing debate and final vote take place at the plenary session.

The Hungarian parliament is one of the fastest to legislate within the EU. The whole parliamentary phase takes only four to five weeks in average, if the ordinary (not accelerated) procedure is used. However, there are possibilities upon qualified majority decision to speed up the process and approve legislation even within two days. The possibility of having a law adopted so quickly often leads to a temptation for politicians to react to societal challenges within quick legislation, usually without thorough preparation and elaboration. The share of laws that were amended within

---

35 Decision no. 10/2014 of the National Assembly on Certain rules of parliamentary procedure.
36 Law on the National Assembly No. 36/2012.

one year of their (original) adoption grew from about 5 to 8 percent (before 2010) to almost 25 percent after 2011.[37]

During parliamentary process, the proposal is being debated and possibly amended in committee and plenary. While opposition MPs seek to change the policy of the proposal, most amendments submitted by governmental MPs rather seek to correct technical mistakes which remained in the bills after the inter-ministerial consultation and controlling phase. Especially the Committee for Legislation has the task to take care of the coherence of the bill, relying on the (confidential) opinion of the legislative department of the parliamentary services.[38] As far as parliamentary debates are concerned, the time reserved for debating bills has been continuously decreasing, and the debates have little or no impact on the outcome. The parliamentary phase of legislation slowly becomes an obligatory but purely formal task in Hungary.[39]

Table 2: The number of recently adopted bills (broken down by proposing subject)

Year	Members of parliament		Cabinet		Committee	
	submitted	adopted	submitted	adopted	submitted	adopted
2010 – 2014	902	269	597	570	22	20
2014 – 2018	744	146	566	564	24	17
2014	114	24	63	70	6	3
2015	231	42	182	181	9	7
2016	224	42	156	148	2	2
2017	175	38	165	165	7	5
2018	116	19	103	113	4	4
2019	86	11	107	114	4	4

Source: Data extracted from www.parlament.hu.

---

37 P Smuk, 'Az Országgyűlés' in J Szerk and G Gajduschek, *A magyar jogrendszer állapota* (MTA TK 2016) 631.
38 During the 1990s it happened that contradicting amendments remained in the final version of the bill after the final vote, which led to another vote or correction by the official gazette.
39 Zs Szabó, 'Hozzáadott érték benyújtás és elfogadás között: viták és módosító javaslatok az Országgyűlésben 2006–2016 között' (2017) Parlamenti Szemle 25-47.

Note: 2014 and 2018 were election years with less parliamentary activity before the elections. The number of these years only shows the activity of the newly elected parliament. Since some bills were submitted by the Cabinet before the elections, Cabinet has higher adoption numbers than submissions.

The afterlife of laws also deserves a short mention. An important feature of the Hungarian legal system is the high number of amendments of recently adopted laws. In some policy areas governed mainly by laws overloaded with detailed provisions (education, health, agriculture etc.), it is common to bring a yearly or sessional 'update package' to parliament packed into a huge set of amendments. These so-called 'salad laws' often modify dozens, or even up to a hundred of other laws, sometimes reflecting changes in relevant EU legislation or consequences of the cross-sectoral reform policies (e.g. e-government), but often only correcting previous wrong drafting or target-setting. Many laws have an already 'scheduled' amendment rate of two to three major amendments per year. This is most obvious at the taxation legislation, which is amended regularly, together with the budget approval. The law amended most times underwent 525 (mostly technical) textual amendments, although it was adopted only in 2011.[40]

While this trend can be partly explained by the structure of the legal system and the even faster changing novelties of our modern times, there are amendments which are aiming at correcting previously made mistakes caused by time pressure. As noted above, the number of laws modified within a year is increasing. The average number of amendments during lifetime of a law reaches 14 and laws are more frequently amended than secondary legislation. The genre of ex-post evaluations, which could support a more consistent framework for ex-post amendments, is strictly voluntary (§ 21 LoL) and in practice almost completely missing in Hungary.[41] Ex-post scrutiny in parliamentary committees is a task in theory, but hardly ever takes place in practice.

---

40 Law no. CXCV/2011 on State finances.
41 Gajduschek 2016, *ibid*, p. 811.

Conclusions

Hungarian legislation can generally be described as quickly adopted, instable and overgrown. A strategic approach for drafting legislation does not exist, neither ex-ante nor ex-post evaluations are given enough weight. The legislative practice is dominated by the daily political agenda, procedural rules tempt politicians to fast reactions to societal problems by legislation instead of using other tools. The formal rules for creating and adopting legislative acts, including those contained in the constitution, are also very flexible. Laws are generally conceived not as instrument of policies (or implementation of Cabinet programme) but as tools to implement single political issue.

Parliament is burdened with legislative tasks, allowing insufficient time for thorough deliberation. Delegated legislation does not have the same importance as statutory one. Formal and institutional guarantees of rule of law (including the activity of the Constitutional Court) are preserved, but quality of legislation lags behind. During legislative drafting, formalities are observed yet impact assessments and consultations are often performed perfunctorily or not at all. Justifications for legislative proposals are regularly prepared (as procedural rules foresee), but the real aim of legislation mostly remains unclear. Constitutional compliance and legislative rules are controlled during the whole drafting process at multiple stages (quality-checking by the MoJ at inter-ministerial consultations, Committee for Legislation in the parliamentary phase), unfortunately strategic questions like 'which kind of legislation is needed' (if any) are hardly raised. Concepts (green papers etc.) are not prepared or consulted, instead, long paragraphed legislative proposals are drafted in the first step of the procedure.

All this lead to the change of legislative roles. In ideal circumstances, politicians define the main targets or concepts of legislation, and the expertise of the ministries define the tools to reach them. The Hungarian practice shows the contrary: very often civil servants define political targets by choosing legislative tools and drafting legal texts, and politicians consequently debate over detailed provisions of legislative proposals.[42] Government's legislation is characterised by political agenda-setting im-

---

42 G Gajduschek 'A közpolitikai célok megjelenése a jogban' in J Szerk and G Gajduschek (eds), *A magyar jogrendszer állapota* (MTA TK 2016).

plemented by legal procedures and expertise, wider policy aspects (societal, sustainability) are often neglected. Despite these deficiencies, the legislative system is still able to handle and coordinate professional and complex procedures, which – in times of constant ongoing policy reforms and increasing quantity of EU-legislation to be transposed – is clearly an advantage.

Poland

Jacek Sokolowski

Introduction: Polish political system and its path dependency

Poland, the first Eastern Europe country to undermine the political monopoly of the communist party, was also the one in which the transition to a fully democratic regime took the longest time. As a result of Round Table Agreement between the ruling United Polish Workers Party (*Polska Zjednoczona Partia Robotnicza, PZPR*) and the oppositional Solidarity movement in 1989 the first free elections were postponed until October 1991. This interim period shaped decisively both the political institutions of the country and the basic socio-political cleavage, namely the one between the supporters of an inclusive transformation model and those of an exclusive one[1] (the latter consisting of demands for decommunization combined with the radical rebuilding of state institutions, and of measures against former nomenklatura appropriating public enterprises). It also allowed the PZPR to transform itself into a nominally social-democratic party which subsequently dominated the political system for a decade (1993-2003). This led to a very gradual and/or superficial reconstruction of institutions inherited from the communist state: public administration, judiciary, and higher education were all functioning within unchanged organisational structures and to a great extent with a very slow and gradual inflow of new people.[2]

---

1 Cf. R David, *Lustration and Transitional Justice. Personnel Systems in the Czech Republic, Hungary, and Poland* (University of Pennsylvania Press 2011) for the models of dealing with the past in transitional democracies and HP Kitschelt, Z Mansfeldova, R Markowski and G Toka, *Post-Communist Party Systems, Competition, Representation, and Inter-Party Cooperation* (Cambridge University Press 1999) for post-communist transformation models and the factors shaping them.
2 Public administration was reformed only on a local level in 1990, whereas new administrative system was created in 1999; first major reform of elementary education was introduced in 1998, of the universities in 2009. The judicial system never underwent a complex institutional reform, some important changes were introduced first in 2011.

The Constitution, adopted in 1997 by all political actors supporting the inclusive transformation was weakly legitimized, as it was accepted in a partly boycotted referendum.[3] This led to a situation, in which basic political foundations of the rule of law were defective: a substantial number of citizens did not identify themselves with the state[4] and the legitimization of judiciary institutions was dubious (as the judges actively violating human rights under the communist rule remained in office). Electoral support for parties openly declaring Third Polish Republic "a handicapped state" and promising to finish the "betrayed revolution of 1989" was always substantial and led eventually to the electoral victory of Law and Order party (Prawo i Sprawiedliwość, PiS).

Transformational path dependency is visible in the law-making particularly in two aspects: ineffective and incoherent institutional solutions and (partly conditioned by the former) a predominance of party decisional bodies over the institutions formally responsible for the legislative process.

Institutional aspects of the legislative process at the governmental level

Legislative planning

Until 2011, Council of Ministers was obliged to prepare a legislative working plan each six months.[5] The plan was drafted in a decentralised manner, as a joint list of proposals submitted by individual ministers.[6] The

---

3 There were 53,45 percent of votes in favour of the new Constitution but the turnout was only 42,86 percent. Two legal acts regarding referendums which were in force at that time (Act on constitutional referendum of 23 April 1992 and the Act on referendums of 29 June 1995) foresaw contradictory provisions with regard to the results: the former did not require any quorum, whereas the latter stipulated that the referendum is binding only if the turnout exceeds 50 percent of all citizens entitled to vote. This controversy was solved by the Supreme Court decision in favour of the referendums validity (sygn. III SW 435/97).
4 Until 2011, Poland had a lowest electoral turnout ratio of all East European countries, on average 47,31 percent in national elections.
5 M Berek, *Rada Ministrów jako organ inicjujący postępowanie ustawodawcze* (C.H. Beck 2017).
6 Regulamin pracy Rady Ministrów, Uchwała nr 49 RM , 19 March 2002 (M.P. 2002.13.221); KH Goetz and R Zubek, 'Government, Parliament and Law-making in Poland' (2007) 13 The Journal of Legislative Studies 517-538.

latter were not obliged to include explanatory documents in their proposals and there were no formal rules directed at establishing a hierarchy or allowing to prioritize the proposed bills. Moreover, the Chancellery of Prime Minister (responsible for technical organisation of the planning process), had no sufficient resources to analyse the proposals with regard to their content or with regard to their expected results and costs. Thus, the formally existing requirement to include a rudimentary RIA in the proposal was effectively not enforced. The Prime Minister's ability to intervene in the planning process was very limited, as he had no formal competence to reject the submitted proposals and his real influence was dependant on his relations with the party faction backing the minister.

The existence of the legislative plan did not restrain the ministers from proposing new bills outside the plan. In fact, the number of bills proposed and drafted by individual ministers (and subsequently adopted by the Council of Ministers) independently of the legislative plan varied between 30 and 70 percent in the years 1998-2004[7] and in years 2008-2010 only between 26 and 52 percent of the legislative plans were implemented.[8]

In 2011, the laws governing legislative planning were amended.[9] 'Legislative plan' turned into 'legislative works list' (*Wykaz prac legislacyjnych*) and was formally discarded as a planning utility. Up to now, *Wykaz* remains a dynamic list of bill proposals that have already been submitted, and is updated each time a new bill is proposed. It seems no coincidence that this definitive acceptance of the ministerial 'feudalisation' marked the beginning of the second term of Civic Platform in the government. The first government of this party (2007-2011) attempted to undertake serious reformative efforts in the areas of judiciary and higher education, whereas the second one became famous for its passive public policy and intensive intraparty factional feuds. On the other hand, Donald Tusk – premier minister and the leader of the Civic Platform at the time – did try to restrict his ministers, if not with regard to the number and the political significance of their bills, at least with regard to their legislative quality.

Already in 2010 Tusk managed to enforce the requirement of Prime Minister's acceptance of any ministerial bill proposed outside the legislative plan. For this acceptance, a positive recommendation of the (concurrently

---

7 Goetz and Zubek 2007, *ibid.*
8 Barometr legislacyjny: analiza wykonania programu prac legislacyjnych Rady Ministrów na II półrocze 2010 r., *Program „Sprawne Państwo"* (Ernst & Young 2011).
9 Berek 2017, *ibid.*

created) Cabinet's legislation programming team (*Zespół programowania prac rządu*) should be mandatory. When the legislative plan lost its programming function and became merely a dynamic list, the programming team was transformed into an evaluation unit within Chancellery of the Prime Minister (Department for legislative planning and impact assessment, currently: Department for impact assessment).[10] Basic procedures were introduced for reviewing the proposals, especially to verify the RIAs, the number of which was gradually growing.[11] From 2013 on, a small number of ministerial proposals began to be rejected (about 3 percent) or returned to its introducer to complete the RIA (about 20 percent).[12] This improvement in the quality of drafting did not coincide with growing ability to plan and programme: bills were submitted to the *Wykaz* after 2013 in the same decentralised way and they almost never referred to strategic programmatic documents of the government.[13]

The drafting process

Most of the formal rules regarding governmental drafting are incorporated in the bylaws of the Council of Ministers (*Regulamin Pracy Rady Ministrów, Regulamin RM*).[14] Technical guidelines for drafting legislation are codified in the order of the Prime Minister (*Zasady techniki prawodawczej*).[15] Prior to 2011 the bill was drafted in the appropriate ministry and it was proposed in form of a legal text. One of the changes to the legislative process introduced by the second Donald Tusk government,

---

10 Recently, the programming team has been reinstated (5 February 2019), while the Department for impact assessment remained within the structure of the Chancellery.

11 In 2014 this department was able to review only about 35 percent proposals of the bills and only about 10 percent of the proposed ministerial orders, A Wołek, *Rząd do remontu, Raport Centrum Analiz Klubu Jagiellońskiego* (Klub Jagiellonski 2015).

12 Wołek 2015, *ibid*; the prerogative of the Prime Minister to reject the proposal outside of the legislative plan was introduced in 2010, see Berek 2017, *ibid.*

13 Wołek 2015, *ibid.*

14 Current version available at the Public Information Bulletin: https://bip.kprm.gov.pl/kpr/bip-rady-ministrow/podstawy-prawne/2516,Regulamin-pracy-Rady-Ministrow.html.

15 Current version available at the Sejm webpage: http://prawo.sejm.gov.pl/isap.nsf/download.xsp/WDU20160000283/O/D20160283.pdf.

was to replace the processing of drafts with the processing of bill objectives (outline of the proposed regulation) at a governmental level. As was often observed, discussing the paragraphed bill can lead to focusing on formalities and meaning of specific provisions and not on political, social or economic goals that are to be achieved through this text. A governmental bill should therefore be principally drafted as an outline of a bill. Drafting a bill without the preliminary phase of an outline should be limited only to the cases in which an appropriate decision of the government as a whole or a decision of the Prime Minister was taken.[16]

Drafting an outline was to be preceded by a regulatory test: identification of the problem to be solved, defining the aim and essence of the planned intervention, preliminary social-, economic and financial analysis, and a comparison with foreign regulations on the subject. The outline of a bill does not contain a legislative text as such. It explains the need for the projected legislation, summarizes the scope and content of regulations already in force and presents the scope and content of the proposed project in a descriptive way. Reports, studies and other expertise on the subject is cited (if available) as well as results of any preliminary consultation (if performed). The outline should refer to the European law (with regard to the conformity of the projected legislation) and should contain at least a rudimentary regulatory impact assessment ex ante (RIA).

Ability to initiate the drafting of an outline of a bill, remained widely decentralised: each individual minister and central organ was entitled to begin the procedure. Concurrently to the first drafting steps, the ministry responsible for the drafting is obliged to submit the project to the legislative works list (*Wykaz prac legislacyjnych*), under the coordination of Cabinet's legislation programming team.

Once the outline is drafted, it enters the consultation stage (to the details, see below). The latter includes public consultation, coordination of positions within Cabinet and enquiries among public bodies affected by the proposal. Within this stage, the outline must be presented to all Cabinet members, the chief of the Chancellery of the Prime Minister and to the Government Legislation Centre (*Rządowe Centrum Legislacyjne*, RCL) and it has to be made publicly available through the governmental legislation online depository (*Rządowy Proces Legislacyjny,* RPL-Service). All

---

16 A Markowska and A Waszyńska, *Rządowy proces legislacyjny – opis procedur* (Rządowe Centrum Legislacji 2014).

documents related to the proposal and produced within consultation-coordination-enquiry stage are also available from the depository.[17] Finally, the outline can be accepted by the Council of Ministers. Should that happen, a centralised governmental legislative unit, RCL, is supposed to be responsible for the drafting of a legislative text.

Drafting reform, introduced in 2011 and described above, was abandoned in 2016 by the government formed by PiS after 2015 election. All the rules providing that bills must be drafted exclusively in the form of an outline remained in force but as a distinct procedure, mandatory only on a direct demand of the Prime Minister. In this way, drafting an outline remained possible but became an exception and since 2016 has effectively ceased to be practiced. Current drafting model is based (again) on the preparation of legal text by the responsible ministry. This text is circulated for consultation both within the government and within the public. This also reduced the role of RCL which lost its status of a central institution responsible for the actual drafting of the legal text and became a consultative organ, empowered to suggest changes to formal redaction of the bill.

Consultation

The Polish Council of Ministers does not debate bills during plenary sessions[18]. These are adopted by consensus, which requires a painstaking intra-governmental consultation stage, during which each minister has a possibility to take stand on the bill. Legally fixed time for delivering comments and remarks is 21 days but it is often disregarded. There is no formal mechanism forcing the ministers to deliver their comments in due time.

Concurrently with the intra-governmental consultation stage, public consultation is performed, again not mandatory, but depending on the decision of the ministry responsible for the draft. Due to the increasing pressure on the subsequent governments, the number of proposals submitted to public consultation grows steadily. Any legal subject can take stand on the bill published in the RPL-Service and the ministry responsible for the bill can invite relevant representatives of the private and the third sector to

---

17 The depository is available at https://legislacja.rcl.gov.pl/.
18 Berek 2017, *ibid.*

bring in their comments and remarks. There is no legally fixed time for public consultation; the ministry responsible for the bill sets the deadline for submitting comments and remarks. A common practice is to set the timeframe extremely short, especially for controversial projects.

The major controversy regarding Polish legislative practice is related not to the frequency of the consultations but to their scope and the way they are performed. *Regulamin Pracy Rady Ministrów* does not prescribe detailed directives for the forms of consultation; they can be performed by addressing chosen institutions or simply by inviting the public to comment on the draft published in the RPL-Service. It became thus a common practice to treat each draft uploaded into the RPL-Service as 'presented for the public consultation'. Such an attitude improves the governmental indices but has little in common with a real consultation process, especially that the deadlines for bringing comments and opinions are usually very short.

Deficits of mandatory public consultation can be – to a certain extent - justified by the existence of mandatory consultation with actors empowered by law to review bills (drafts) within relevant scope of regulation. This particular corporationist trait of Polish legislative process grants consultation rights to trade unions and professional corporations and has no universal model, i.e. the privileges of particular actors rely on special provisions of legal acts related to their activity. In particular, all proposals having direct impact on the labour market should be presented for the consultation to the trade unions representing more than 300.000 employees.[19] Free professions, especially the legal ones, enjoy similar privilege. The impact of these corporationist actors on the contents of legislation varies, depending on their actual political strength.

Final drafting, legal editing

Once the consultation stage is closed, the draft is proceeded by the Permanent Ministerial Committee, consisting of one minister (presiding), vice-ministers from every ministry and two representatives of the Prime Minister. The committee's task is to evaluate the comments and remarks presented during the consultation stage and not accepted (or rejected) by the

---

19 Trade Unions Act of 1991, Ustawa z dnia 23 maja 1991 r. o związkach za-wodowych.

ministry responsible for the draft. The draft submitted to the Committee must include RIA-ex ante and the drafts of decisive executive (ministerial) orders which are to be issued after the bill will be passed.

The last stage before the bill would be accepted by the Council of Ministers is the Juridical Committee which agrees the final draft of the legal text. The Juridical Committee is an ad-hoc body, created for each proposal by the head of the RCL and consisting of lawyers delegated by the relevant ministries (i.e. the ministries participating in the intra-governmental consultations), presided by the RCL-delegate.[20] In this final form the draft becomes the subject of decision of the Council of Ministers.

Several auxiliary bodies might be be included in the inter-governmental drafting process, namely European Committee, Digitalisation Committee, Economic Committee and the Legislative Council. Each of them reviews drafts falling into their scope of competence after the consultation stage is closed and before the final version approved by the Juridical Committee. The European Committee is responsible for reviewing all governmental documents related to the membership in the EU, which includes the drafts of implementation bills. Digitalisation Committee, mainly responsible for the digitalisation of public administration, reviews relevant drafts. Economic Committee, created in 2016, shall serve as a body coordinating the implementation of Strategy for Responsible Development, a major governmental economic strategy. It has therefore a potential (and formal competence) to intervene in the intragovernmental drafting process, but its real impact has been weak.

Finally, the Legislative Council is an auxiliary body created as early as 1972,[21] whose main function was to control the legislative quality of major legal acts (such as codices) and which was (traditionally) composed of most respected legal experts, nominated by the Premier Minister. Still existing, its competences cross with those of Juridical Committee and also, of the RCL, especially that the opinion of the Council is usually requested at the early consultation stage, when the final text had not been yet agreed

---

20 § 71-78 Regulamin Pracy Rady Ministrów, *ibid.*
21 Currently, the Legislative Council is governed by the provisions of the Ministers' Council Act (Ustawa o Radzie Ministrów, Dz.U. 1996 Nr 106, poz. 492, t.j. Dz.U. z 2019 r. poz. 1171), the Prime Ministers' Decree on the Legislative Council (Rozporządzenie Prezesa Rady Ministrów w sprawie zadań Rady Legislacyjnej oraz szczegółowych zasad i trybu jej funkcjonowania, Dz.U. 2011 Nr 6, poz. 21), and by the Regulamin Pracy Rady Ministrów, *ibid.*

upon by all members of the Council of Ministers. Its real impact is very limited, particularly by the current Prime Ministers' Decree on the Legislative Council, according to which Legislative Council's opinion is not mandatory. It consults the proposals only upon the request of the Prime Minister, of the chief of the Permanent Ministerial Committee, the chief of the RCL or of the chief of the Prime Ministers' Chancellery. What is more, according to the § 2 of the Decree, Legislative Council is to be called upon only to consult 'particularly significant proposals' and the proposals arousing controversies with regard to their constitutional conformity, which limits further the number of drafts examined by this body.[22]

Unclear competences' division between the Juridical Committee, the Legislative Council and the RCL explain to a certain extent poor quality and incoherence of many legal acts. Developed historically to serve (partly) overlapping functions, these three bodies do not have currently a clearly formulated scope of competence.

Regulatory impact assessment

The true RIA system has not been fully implemented in Poland yet, though first attempts date back to 2002 when it was mentioned for the first time in regulations of the Council of Ministers.[23] The first comprehensive guidelines for performing RIA were created in 2006 by the Ministry of Economy (*Wytyczne 2006*) but their use was not obligatory. Only after 2011, due to the reform of legislative process undertaken by the second Tusk government, formal measures to enforce mandatory RIA ex ante appeared together with the growing tendency among ministries to conform to this requirement, especially as the role of the Cabinet's legislation programming team and of the Department for Impact Assessment in the Prime Minister Chancellery was of substantial importance.

In 2013, a governmental programme "Better Regulations 2015" was adopted, with the proclaimed aim to achieve Western standards in the governmental drafting process by 2015. In 2014, new guidelines for RIA were

---

22 Between 2010 and 2014, Legislative Council consulted in total 59 proposals, cf. *Sprawozdanie z działalności Rady Legislacyjnej przy Prezesie Rady Ministrów (XI kadencja – od 29 czerwca 2010 r. do 29 czerwca 2014 r.)* (2014) Przegląd Legislacyjny 101.

23 Uchwała nr 49 Rady Ministrów z 19 marca 2002 r; M.P. nr 13, poz. 221.

adopted by the government, integrating both the 2006 guidelines and two manuals regarding the consultation process (*Wytyczne 2015*). In this way, a comprehensive administrative manual was created, the contents of which were mostly evaluated very positively by the experts.[24] According the latter guidelines, regulatory impact assessment (*Ocena Wpływu, OW*) consists of the following steps:

- Regulatory test (*Test regulacyjny, TR*): performed mandatory before launching the drafting of the outline of the bill (or the legal draft);
- RIA ex ante (*Ocena skutków regulacji, OSR*): prepared mandatory for the drafted legal text;
- RIA ex post (*OSR ex post*): prepared optionally by the ministry responsible for drafting the bill after it was passed by the parliament and went in force.

Additionally, modified *Regulamin RM* strengthened the role of RIA, creating a position of RIA-coordinator, who can be appointed by Prime Minister for particular bill proposals. Otherwise Chief of the Prime Minister's Chancellery is responsible for RIA coordination on a permanent basis. He can block the consultation stage until RIA-ex ante has been performed. Opinion of the RIA-coordinator is however, not mandatory for each proposal but only in the cases when the Cabinet's legislation programming team (*Zespół programowania prac rządu*) puts forward such motion.

As mentioned above, the model of governmental legislative process created before 2015 was effectively abandoned in 2016. The requirements regarding RIA remained admittedly in force, however the determination to fully implement the model introduced in *Wytyczne 2015* has decreased. Moreover, negative practice of introducing ministerial drafts to the Parliament via deputies from the governing party (previously existing but not widespread) increased rapidly since the PiS Government was formed after 2015 elections.[25] One of the reasons was the desire to bypass the time-consuming intra-governmental consultation and to loosen the public control over the proposals. Especially the latter was the obvious reason with

---

24 J Górniak (ed), *Ocena wpływu oparta na dowodach. Model dla Polski* (Akademia Leona Koźmińskiego 2015).

25 M Dzieciuch, 'Ocena polskiego procesu legislacyjnego na przykładzie ostatnich zmian w prawie rynków finansowych' (2018) 7 Internetowy Kwartalnik Antymonopolowy i Regulacyjny 8-20.

regard to the proposals of bills regulating the judiciary which were often very controversial and proceeded at high-speed.

Recent report of the Supreme Chamber of Control shows that in four key ministries (Finance, Social & Labour, Agriculture, Development) in the years 2015-2016 only 30 percent of the proceeded projects were drafted in accordance with the RIA-guidelines.[26]

The practice of drafting and its political context

Decentralised manner in which the legislative agenda is created and in which the proposals are proceeded reflects the weak degree of institutionalisation of Polish political parties. Polish party scene stabilised around 2007 when the hitherto domination of the post-communist *Sojusz Lewicy Demokratycznej (SLD)*[27] ended. During the period 2007 – 2015 major political rivals were two post-Solidarity parties: PiS and Civic Platform (*Platforma Obywatelska,* PO), A majority of their members entered politics mostly after 2005.[28] PiS and PO were both founded around 2000/2001 and experienced an intense growth from 2005 onwards. It took them several years to develop a relatively stable internal party structure. In case of PO, this process was already advanced in the second term of Donald Tusk (2011-2015), which explains why it was his government who undertook in 2011 a major reform of the legislative process, aimed at restricting the ministerial 'feudalisation', and at strengthening the coordination role played by the Prime Minister's Chancellery and the RCL. After 2015 however, victorious PiS took over, bringing in new people with little polit-

---

26 Supreme Chamber of Control, Report on RIA 2017 (NIK o dokonywaniu oceny wpływu w ramach rządowego procesu legislacyjnego, 2017) available from https://www.nik.gov.pl/aktualnosci/nik-o-dokonywaniu-oceny-wplywu-w-nbsp-ramach-rzadowego-procesu-legislacyjnego.html.

27 Post-communist meaning here a party created by the former member of communist party and representing the economic and political interests of the beneficiaries of the former regime in the transformation society.

28 Of all the *Sejm* deputies in 2013, 24,4 percent were politicians first elected in 2005, 17,4 percent in 2007, 18,4 percent in 2011, cf. R Matyja and B Sajduk, *Polska elita polityczna 2013* (WSE Kraków 2014).

ical experience not only to strictly political positions but also to the public administration.[29]

Within the past four years, PiS transformed itself from a relatively small cadre-party with very limited local establishment (PiS was ruling only in very few local governments and in none of the 16 regional governments) into a state-wide conglomerate of political factions and interest-groups intertwined with factions within public administration and other social and economic stakeholders on every level of government (especially after 2018 local elections, in which PiS took power in eight out of 16 regions).This makes intra-party dynamics very intense, especially taking into consideration that in fact government lead by Prime Minister Morawiecki consists of three, formally independent coalition partners.[30] The coordination possibilities of the Prime Minister are thus very limited, especially taking into account that the party leader, Jarosław Kaczyński, declines to enter the government and reserves for himself the role of a 'man in the shadow'. This leads to a situation, in which the man formally responsible for political leadership and agenda setting, i.e. the Prime Minister, does not have at his disposal the real instruments allowing him to control the party. On the other hand, Jarosław Kaczyński controls the PiS and can informally impose direction of the major political undertakings of the government. However, he has access neither to the instruments necessary to perform the 'everyday governing' nor to the instruments allowing to monitor the enactment of the governmental strategies. Combined with the above-mentioned intra party dynamics, conditioned by thousands of people competing for a better position within the unstable party structure informing, this creates perfect conditions for a feudalisation of policy-making.

The effort to centralise and coordinate the policy areas regarded as crucial by the ruling party have indeed been undertaken, however mostly through informal measures and not through building or strengthening le-

---

29 From 2016 onwards, in total more than 11000 officials were removed from their posts in public administration, see J Paczocha, *Partia w Państwie: Bezprecedensowa wymiana kadr w administracji rządowej i jej legislacyjne podstawy* (FOR 2018).

30 The alliance called United Right, *Zjednoczona Prawica* consists of PiS, *Solidarna Polska* and *Polska Razem*. Their constituencies differ enough to offer each of the smaller partners a chance to exceed the electoral threshold, therefore their position with the alliance leaves them a certain degree of autonomy.

gislative institutions. Ministers responsible for these areas enjoyed autonomy in drafting and were clearly protected from interventions of other ministers during the consultation stage. This was visible especially with regard to:

- Fiscal reforms in 2017 (fighting the VAT-abuses and tightening the fiscal system), minister responsible: Mateusz Morawiecki.[31]
- Reform of higher education, minister responsible: Jarosław Gowin.
- Controversial changes in the judiciary system, minister responsible: Zbigniew Ziobro.

First of these proposals was accepted by the Sejm without any major changes, thanks to the tight control executed over the party by Jarosław Kaczyński, Morawiecki's political protector. The other two were amended – the Higher Education Act during parliamentary proceedings (as a result of a serious intra-party controversy, from which Kaczynski distanced himself but pressed major Gowin's opponents into a compromise) and the 'judiciary reform' was vetoed by the President, which led to negotiations between him and the party leader, on grounds of which new drafts were proposed by the Ministry of Justice. These three examples prove that informal consultation mechanism and Kaczynski's influence executed on his party remain major factors determining the content of legislative proposals with regard to important policy areas.

In cases in which this influence was missing, especially in those where regulation subject was complex and/or required long-term cooperation between various government branches, the legislative process stalled. This lack of ability to coordinate the activity and interests of different ministers is clearly visible in the areas of tax law, transport infrastructure and health care, in which the ruling party abandoned all more ambitious projects of a complex reform.[32]

In clear contrast to the above remain proposals falling into competence of one ministry and not requiring particular cooperation within government. They are usually proceeded very fast, with only a superficial *quasi-RIA*. Their authors also tend to ignore public consultation, mostly through

---

31 At that time Minister of Finance, Mateusz Morawiecki, became Prime Minister in December 2017.
32 Based on yearly reports of Klub Jagielloński, an independent think-tank evaluating public policy, see for example T Ociepki et al (eds), *Rząd pod lupą. Ranking polityk publicznych 2018* (Klub Jagiellonski 2019).

extreme shortening of the time dedicated for it.[33] Although exact data are not available, the number of proposals drafted by ministerial bureaucracy and formally proposed as a parliamentary draft by a group of deputies is growing rapidly after 2015.[34]

Conclusion

Main feature of the Polish legislative proceedings at the governmental level was – and remains – its 'feudalisation', i. e. lack of coordination between single members of the government and relative autonomy of ministers within areas belonging to their competence. During the second term of Tusk government, a substantial effort was put into institutional restructuring of the governmental law-making. Instruments were created which allowed the Prime Minister to exercise formal influence on the public policy by means of examining the content of ministerial proposals. Combined with party leadership of the Prime Minister, this allowed to strengthen the cohesion of public policy. This idea was clearly abandoned after 2015. Major legislative proposals which had informal backing of the party leader were pressed through the process of governmental drafting thanks to informal influence of Jaroslaw Kaczynski. At the same time less important (in political terms) projects were either abandoned because of institutional inability to proceed them, or were ceded to appropriate ministers with a substantial degree of autonomy.

---

33 G Kopińska, 'Rządowy proces legislacyjny' (2015) Analiza Programu Odpowiedzialne Panstwo 1-5.
34 In this way, RIA-*ex ante* can be avaided, as it is not required from parliamentary drafts, cf. Dzieciuch 2018, *ibid.*

The Slovak Republic

Milan Hodas

Introduction

Law-making in the Slovak Republic complies with the current trend characterized by the fact that a substantial part is performed at the executive level.[1] In the sense of the idea that "who does the work, has the influence", with the increasing role/dominance of the executive in the field of law-making, its influence is also increasing in general.[2] Although the factual status of the parliament is weakened, it is still constitutionally significant as it reflects the pursuit of democratic processes. It is generally known that law-making in a democracy and the rule of law is to be built upon the principles of pluralism[3] involving active participation of public.[4] Pluralism as a modus operandi based on the idea of disputes and conflicts, as well as on the idea of correct, structured and systematic dispute settlement between the set of institutions that make up the state, i.e. between the executive, legislative, judiciary and between the different levels of the administrative hierarchy, whether at the vertical or horizontal levels, as well as between political and the bureaucratic apparatus,[5] is negatively influenced by the deformations and nepotism, political patronage, corruption, and so on. This also inevitably has a negative influence on law-making. Situation in the Slovak Republic is no exception in its quest for efficient

---

1 B Balog, *Umenie tvoriť zákony, Schvaľovanie zákonov v Slovenskej republike* (Wolters Kluwer 2019) 48-49.

2 As writes Pier Ferdinando Casini „... in many countries parliament – the central institution of democracy – is facing a crisis of legitimacy.", see D Beetham, *parliament and democracy in the twenty – first century, a guide to good practice* (Interparliamentary Union 2006) 4.

3 O Escobar, 'Pluralism and Democratic Participation: What Kind of Citizen are Citizens Invited to Be?' (2017) 14 Contemporary Pragmatism 416-438.

4 J Plichtová, 'Občianska deliberatívna demokracia a podpora jej cieľov na Slovensku' (2010) 42 Sociológia 516-547.

5 Compare with K Staroňová and L Malíková, 'The view of political science on the phenomenon of corruption' (2007) 39 Sociológia 287.

democratic law-making. It faces abovementioned problems and tries to deal with them.

It is not only constitutional set up and political practice that influence the law-making in Slovakia. There are only few legislators and even fewer good legislators. At the beginning of the existence of the independent Slovak Republic it was caused by the fact that in 1993 many quality legislators remained in the Czech Republic.[6] Moreover, in relation of the Slovak Republic's accession process to the European Union, Deputy Prime Minister Jozef Kalman pointed out the lack of foreign language-equipped legislators.[7] In 2014 an analysis aimed at monitoring of the administrative and regulatory burdens on business drew attention to the lack of quality legislators in individual ministries, due to the exchange of people by the new governments after parliamentary elections.[8] The shortage of capable legislators is still visible nowadays.[9] Moreover, practical experience shows that even the legislators of the highest-quality may not always be capable of influencing the (wrong) political purpose. After the revolution in 1989, the transition to democratic pluralistic creation of public policies was also marked by the authoritarian periods of the ruling of Vladimir Mečiar.[10] Politics, interest groups and oligarchs have influenced, and will always lawfully or unlawfully influence legislative process. However, at the same time there has been evolving activity of the civil society, namely through participation in commenting on bills, which has also been reflected in law-making. Employers and employees' representatives are also purposefully involved in creation of public policies. This is the aim of Act No. 103/2007 Coll. on Tripartite Consultations at the National Level (Tripar-

---

6 In the parliamentary debate, this was pointed out by deputy K. Tóthová in 2002. Available at http://www.psp.cz/eknih/1998nr/stenprot/062schuz/s062009.htm.

7 Available at https://www.sme.sk/c/2120038/prihlaska-slovenska-za-clena-eu-do-30-juna.html.

8 C Roman et al, *Analýza, monitor merania administratívneho a regulačného zaťaženia podnikania* (Centrum vzdelávania MPSVR SR 2014) 106.

9 See for example M Mamojka, 'Normotvorná a aplikačná stránka zákonnosti ako sinergia právneho štátu' in M Turošík and A Ševčiková (eds), *Banskobystrické dni práva na tému „Kvalita normotvornej a aplikačnej stránky zákonnosti ako determinant právneho štátu* (Belianum 2017) 7.

10 See S Somolányi, 'Slovakia: From a Difficult Case of Transition to a Consolidated Central European Democracy' in T Hayashi (ed), *Democracy and Market Economics in Central and Eastern Europe: Are New Institutions Being Consolidated?* (SRC 2004) 149-188.

tite Act), which already in § 1 declares that its aim is to promote effective social dialogue at the national level between the state and employers with employees ("social partners") through their representatives as a democratic means of solving economic and social development, development of employment and assuring social peace.

The Slovak political and constitutional system and its effects on law-making

The law-making (drafting of bills) is significantly determined by the constitutional set-up of relations between the government, the parliament, the president, as well as by the specific political circumstances and rules of the legislative processes.

In case of the Slovak Republic, one may speak of a parliamentary republic.[11] According to the Constitution of the Slovak Republic (hereinafter "Constitution"), the sole legislative and constitutional body of the Slovak Republic is the National Council of the Slovak Republic (hereinafter "NC SR"),[12] a unicameral parliament composed of 150 Members (Art. 72 of the Constitution).[13] Constitutionally defined is also the right of legislative initiative. Bills may only be introduced by the committees of the NC SR, deputies of the NC SR and the government (Art. 87 of the Constitution). The president cannot initiate legislation. Pursuant to Art. 87(3) of the Constitution, the act shall be signed by the president, the Speaker of the NC SR and the Prime Minister before the promulgation. The signing of the law by the Prime Minister and the speaker of the parliament is rather of ceremonial significance and does not constitute consent to its content.[14]

The president disposes with the right of a suspensive relative veto. This means that the president can return an approved law with comments to the NC SR within 15 days of delivery of the approved law [see Art. 102 (1) (o) of the Constitution]. This presidential veto can be "overridden" by the vote of an absolute majority of all deputies of the NC SR [76 Members;

---

11 See A Bröstl et al, *Ústavné právo Slovenskej republiky* (Aleš Čeněk 2010) 217.

12 F Korn, *Objektívne právo ako spoločenský normatívny system* (Tribun EU 2019) 105; see also M Giba et al, *Ústavné pravo* (Wolters Kluwer 2019) 169.

13 L Cibulka et al, *Ústavné právo, Ústavný systém Slovenskej republiky* (Univerzita Komenského 2014) 223 et seq.

14 B Fábry, *Teoretické problémy tvorby práva* (A-Medi management 2018) 208.

Art. 86 (3) of the Constitution] during the repeated adoption of the law.[15] After the (second) adoption succeeds, the president can no longer veto the law. The president has no right to veto the constitutional law.[16] In practice the president is sometimes asked by the deputies of the NC SR to veto the bill in cases if the hectic process of passing the bill lead to serious legislative errors. There are also cases where there is a vocal demand on the president to veto the bill.[17]

The Constitutional Court of the Slovak Republic acts as a so-called "negative legislator" by carrying out the review of the constitutionality of the approved laws (ex-post control, Art. 125 of the Constitution).[18] Thus, it does not possess the power of ex-ante review of conformity of the bills with the Constitution. This role is exercised by the Legislative Council of the government of the Slovak Republic[19] as well as by the Constitutional Affairs Committee of the NC SR, which has the duty to discuss all draft laws that have reached the second reading [§ 59 b) of the Act No. 350/1996 Coll. on the Rules of Procedure of the National Council of the Slovak Republic].

If the Constitutional Court decides in the ex-post review that there is inconsistency between the law(s) under review and the Constitution, constitutional laws, international treaties, then the whole law or selected provisions from that law under review become ineffective. The bodies that issued these legal regulations are obliged to ensure, within six months from promulgation of the decision of the Constitutional Court, their compliance with the Constitution, constitutional laws and international treaties. If they fail to do so, the validity of such regulations, their parts or provisions shall

---

15 See J Drgonec, *Ústava Slovenskej republiky, Teória a prax* (C. H. Beck 2015) 1210.
16 Drgonec 2015, *ibid*, p. 1138.
17 For example in September 2019 Reporters Without Borders asked Slovak president Zuzana Čaputova to veto bill extending politicians' right of reply. Available at https://rsf.org/en/news/slovak-president-urged-veto-extending-politicians-right-reply.
18 See B Balog and A Bonko, 'Legislatívne nič a ústavný súd' (2012) 4 Notitiae ex Academia Bratislavensi Iurisprudentiae 9, see also B Šramel, *Ústavné súdnictvo* (Občianske združenie FSV 2015) 47.
19 See J Svák et a., *Teória a prax legislatívy* (Eurokódex 2012) 116-117.

terminate six months from the promulgation of the decision [Art. 125 (3) of the Constitution].[20]

Preparation of draft bills at the executive level – legal and institutional framework

When writing about preparation of bills at the executive level, we have to mention Act No. 575/2001 Coll. on "Organization of the activity of the government and on the organization of the central state administration". This law sets out the basic characteristics of the government's activities. The governmental sessions are not public, this however does not affect the government's duty to inform the public on the result of the sessions (e.g. to publish legislative materials and non-legislative materials on the government's webpage).[21] The cited law also stipulates that tasks connected with the professional, organizational and technical provision of the government's activities are performed by the Office of the Government of the Slovak Republic. Other parts of the law contain the definition of competences of individual ministries or central state administration bodies.

Additionally, pursuant to § 37 of Act No. 575/2001 Coll., ministries and other central state administration bodies are responsible for proper legal regulation of matters falling within their competence. Thus, they have a legal obligation to prepare bills and other generally binding legal regulations, to publish the drafts to enable the comments by the public and to submit them to the government after the exchange of views in the interdepartmental comments procedure (see below). Finally, the ministries and other central state administration bodies have an obligation to use the knowledge of public institutions, scientific institutions, research institutions and professional and trade organizations and engage them in the work of dealing with issues of conceptual and legislative nature.

An important legal standard laying down the requirements that generally binding legal acts must meet is Act No. 400/2015 Coll. on "Creation of

---

20 Details in T Ľalík, 'Všeobecné a individuálne účinky derogačných nálezov Ústavného súdu SR' (2018) 70 Justičná revue 711-732.

21 The duty of the government to publish materials submitted on the government's meeting results from the § 5 (4) of the Act No. 211/2000 Coll. (Freedom of Information Act), see P Wilfling, *Zákon o slobodnom prístupe k informáciám, komentár, problémy z praxe, rozhodnutia súdov* (Via Iuris 2015) 205.

legal regulations and on the Collection of Laws of the Slovak Republic. This law determines the material and procedural aspects for the creation of generally binding legal regulations. For instance, it is stipulated that the creation of a draft of a generally binding legal regulation and its attachments[22] takes place at the designated legislation portal.[23] The portal is part of "Slov-Lex" public administration information system, administered and operated by the Ministry of Justice. Part of this web portal is a legislative editor through which the drafting processes should be carried out.[24] Its use is however often not effective for various reasons, such as the unwillingness to change the "traditional" procedures for the preparation of legislative materials or fluctuation of legislators that precludes creation of stabilized core of experienced legislative staff.[25]

Regarding the content of a draft of a generally binding legal regulation, it can be said that during preparation of bills, the government proceeds in accordance with so-called Plan of Legislative Tasks approved for a particular year. This plan is based on a so-called Framework Plan of the Legislative Tasks of the Government, while this Framework Plan is linked to manifesto which the government presents in the NC SR during the investiture vote. The government may also prepare a draft bill that is not included in the plans, if required by the urgency of the situation.

An important part of law-making are interactions with the public and public administration bodies, which did not immediately participate in the drafting of bills, is the so-called Preliminary Information Procedure and the Interdepartmental Comments Procedure.[26] Prior to launching the drafting of a bill, the proposer publishes the preliminary information on the bill that is being prepared on the portal in order to inform the public bodies. The proposer briefly outlines the fundamental aims and the theoretical background of the bill that is being prepared, the assessment of the current

---

22 For example statement of legislative intent, explanatory statement, analysis of impact, report on public participation in creating the legislation, table of compliance of the generally binding legal regulation with the EU Law.
23 See also J Svák, Ž Surmajová and B Balog, *Zákon o tvorbe právnych predpisov a o Zbierke zákonov Slovenskej republiky: Komentár* (Wolters Kluwer 2017) 84-86.
24 K Baraník, 'Legislatívny proces v Slovenskej republike a jeho digitalizácia' in E Žatecká et al (eds) *Cofola: conference proceedings* (Masarykova univerzita 2011) 1572-1586.
25 See for example, also J Svák and B Balog, 'Legislatívna kultúra' (2018) 101 Právny obzor 358-359.
26 See details in Svák et al 2012, *ibid*, p. 156.

situation and the expected date of commencement of the Interdepartmental Comments Procedure (see § 9 of Act No. 400/2015 Coll.). The draft itself is subsequently published on the portal for the Interdepartmental Comments Procedure. The commenting is carried out on the portal in a way to ensure the possibility for public to comment on the draft. Only contributions which are exercised within the given time frame and unambiguously formulated and justified can be accepted as a comment to the bill.

The Legislative Directive of the government includes legislative and technical requirements for bills. In respect to the Interdepartmental Comments Procedure, the Legislative Directive stipulates that apart from publication on portal, the proposer must also send an electronic notice of publication of the draft bill to the so-called compulsory commentators:

- deputy prime ministers, ministries and other central state administration bodies,
- Office of the Government – Section of Government Legislation – the Department of Approximation of Law,
- National Bank of Slovakia,
- Supreme Audit Office of the Slovak Republic,
- Supreme Court of the Slovak Republic,
- General Prosecutors Office of the Slovak Republic,
- representatives of employers and representatives of employees, in case of a bill concerning economic and social interests, as well as other bodies and institutions, as provided for in a special regulation or designated by the government [Art. 13(2) of Legislative Directive].

The interdepartmental comments procedure to a bill is also carried out with higher territorial units, the Association of self-governing regions SK 8, the Association of towns and communities of Slovakia, the Union of towns and cities of Slovakia, the capital city of Slovakia – Bratislava, cities with the seat of the region and bodies and institutions charged with tasks or concerned with the topic of the bill, as well as with the public [Art. 13(3) of Legislative Directive]. The proposer may also send a notice of publication of the draft to other state bodies, local government authorities, professional organizations and other institutions [Art. 13(4) of Legislative Directive].

The notice of publication of the bill includes its title, the start and the end date of the Interdepartmental Comments Procedure, the deadline for sending the comments, the link to the exact location of the material on the portal and the email address to which comments may be sent if the portal is unavailable.

The standard deadline for submission of comments is 15 working days, if the proposer does not specify a longer period; the period for submission starts running from the first date of publication of the bill on the portal. If the commenting body or institution fails to send the comments within the specified time frame, it is considered that it has no objection [Art. 13(6) of Legislative Directive].

If exceptional circumstances exist,[27] if there is a risk of non-fulfillment of the obligations arising from the Treaty of accession of the Slovak Republic to the European Union by failing to meet the deadline for implementation of EU law, or if it concerns a bill submitted outside the Plan of Legislative Tasks due to its urgency within a deadline that does not allow for complying with a 15-day deadline, the Interdepartmental Comments Procedure may be shortened. In this case, the deadline for submission of comments is set by the proposer, however, this deadline shall not be shorter than seven working days and shall start running on the day of publication of the bill on the portal [Art. 13(7) of Legislative Directive].

In practice proposers often fail to comply with the set deadline, or they use time periods when there is an assumption that the material will receive lower attention of the public (e.g. summer holidays, Christmas holidays). New provision or modification of the existing provisions could be proposed within the Interdepartmental Comments Procedure. Even proposals that contain specific reservations to the text of the bill or pointing to certain shortcoming of the bill are considered as comments (Art. 10 of Act No. 400/2015 Coll.). Initiatives which do not meet these criteria do not have to be taken into account by the proposer. The refusal to accept comment which was made by the so-called compulsory commentators (ministries and other central state administration bodies) or the refusal to accept a comment submitted by at least 500 people leads to the so-called dispute settling procedure. Further details on the dispute settling procedure are set forth by the Legislative Directive.

A special instrument serving the public is a system developed in relation to the enrolment of the government into the Open Government Partnership, a so-called electronic bulk request. The electronic bulk request is

---

27 In particular, if there is a threat to human rights and fundamental freedoms or the safety of citizens, or a threat of significant financial damage to state, or in the event of declaration of state emergency.

a voluntary commitment by the government to deal with every initiative/ request that can collect 15 000 signatures electronically within 30 days. This commitment of the government was adopted by Resolution of the Government of the Slovak Republic No. 636/2015 from 25 November 2015. If the request receives 15 000 signatures, the system administrator (the Office of the Government) designates the subject responsible for preparing the necessary material for governmental session. The proposal for a solution of the bill reflecting the requirements of the request must be submitted by the responsible subject to the governmental session within 90 days of the assembly of signatures. The government shall take a decision in the form of a resolution on the submitted bill drawn up upon the initiative of the electronic bulk request and may delegate to the competent minister or the head of other central state administration body other tasks concerning the submitted material. Surprisingly only one request has been submitted in three years since the system was introduced and it did not meet the necessary formal requirements. Practical experience with this system therefore does not exist. In a special evaluation report on open governance, the expert stated that the reason for not using the electronic bulk request was the high number of signatures required and the necessity to use an electronic identity card.[28]

The quality of law-making increases with the existence of specialized advisory bodies, such as the Legislative Council of the government. The Legislative Council is a permanent advisory and coordinating body of the government in the field of legislature. The legal basis for its existence is the already cited Act No. 575/2001 Coll. [§ 2(3)]. Details on tasks, composition and deliberations of the Legislative Council are stipulated in the statute adopted by the government in the form of a resolution.[29] The Legislative Council is composed of the president, vice-president, secretary and other members. The function of the President of the Legislative Council is exercised by the Deputy Prime Minister for Legislation [§ 4(2) of the Resolution]. Other members of the Legislative Council are appointed and recalled by the government on the basis of the proposal of the president of the Legislative Council, usually from distinguished personalities among legislators, attorneys, judges or academic professionals. The Legislative Council mainly:

---

28 M Žuffová, *Slovenská republika: špeciálna hodnotiaca správa 2014 – 2015* (Iniciatíva pro otvorené vládnutí 2016) 64.

29 Resolution of the government No. 620 from 7 November 2012.

- discusses the annual draft of the Plan of the Legislative Tasks of the Government;
- coordinates and directs the activities of the ministries and other central state administration bodies concerning the preparation of the bills;
- discusses and assesses constitutional bills and statutory bills and draws positions on these proposals;

Assesses the compliance of discussed bills with the EU law and international treaties with which the Slovak Republic is bound.

Legislative Council's discussions are usually held once every 14 days. In urgent cases, the President of the Legislative Council may also call for an extraordinary session of the Legislative Council. What may be problematic is the fact that materials for the Legislative Council's discussions are not always presented sufficiently in advance. In practice, this means that the members of the Legislative Council cannot always assess the materials effectively and in necessary details.

The immanent part of the bills' preparatory process is RIA. First requirements for RIA were introduced in Slovakia already in November 2001 via an amendment of the Legislative Rules, following recommendations by the Audit of State Administration.[30] At present, the assessment of regulatory impacts in Slovakia is fulfilled through the "Unified methodology for the assessment of selected impacts" approved by the Resolution of the government No. 24/2015 with effect from 1 October 2015. Section on selected impacts and analysis of impacts is an obligatory part of any bill [§ 7 of the Act No. 400/2015 Coll.]. The proposing subject shall evaluate the impacts of the bill on the state budget, parenthood and family, business environment, social impacts, environmental impacts, impacts on the informatization of society and effects on public administration services for the citizens. The Permanent Working Committee of the Legislative Council for the Assessment of Selected Impacts at the Ministry of Economy is responsible for the proper evaluation of quality of the impact assessments.

Final stage of the legislative process at the executive level is the meeting of the government. The government decides on bills at a joint meeting.

---

30 K Staroňová, 'Regulatory Impact Assessment: Formal Institutionalization and Practice' (2010) 30 Journal of Public Policy 120-121.

Based on Art. 119 of the Constitution per rollam voting on bills is excluded.[31] The government has a quorum if more than one-half of its members are present. The subject proposing the bill shall introduce the material on the agenda with introductory words (§ 7 of the Rules of Procedure of the government, Resolution of the government No. 512/2001). After the debate and the Prime Minister shall submit the proposal for a decision, taking into account the opinions presented in the debate (§ 9 of the Rules of Procedure) .The consent of more than one-half of government members is necessary to pass a resolution on the bill (Art. 118 of the Constitution).[32]

Practical functioning of the drafting and negotiating process

The factors of time, institutional capacity and political purpose play an important role in law-making. The preparation of bills by the ministries or other bodies of central state administration is affected by their internal structure, work methodology as well as the quality of the staffing and the length of institutional memory.

At selected ministries, we recognize a so-called centralized model of law-making,[33] when a bill is written at a material department (department occupied by experts in the field of the proposed legislation) and subsequently transferred to a legislative department (department employing lawyers specialized in drafting). The legislative department is thus the lead department responsible for the draft. The centralized model of law-making is employed for example by the Ministry of Justice.

There is also a decentralized model of legislative work on draft legislation. In this case the proposal is drawn up to the final version at a material department, which may (but frequently does not) employ legislators besides material experts. However, it is problematic if there are not any qualified legislators working at the material department. Though the bill might be based on knowledge of highly skilled experts, it often contains legislative deficiencies. The decentralized model of law-making is employed for example by the Ministry of Education, Science, Research and Sport.

It is also possible that the same ministry combines both models depending on the content of the bill. Regardless of whether it is a centralized or

---

31 Drgonec 2015, *ibid*, p. 1279.
32 See Fábry 2018, *ibid*, p. 199.
33 See Svák and Kukliš 2012, *ibid*, p. 115.

decentralized model of law-making, it is possible to talk about an eternal tension between legislators and "factualists". While legislators usually have legislative or technical objections touching on the affected objective defined by the factualists, the latter often do not understand the former group and blame the legislators for endangering the intended purpose of the law.

In addition to the aforementioned models, sometimes the legislative work is outsourced and the bill is drafted by a law firm.[34] This is usually the case when a minister does not trust internal employees of his institution. The disadvantage of such practice is that no institutional memory will be created in the given body of state administration and substantial part of both material and legislative know-how will remain in the law firm. Also problematic is the practice when part of the legislative process at the government level is circumvented and the bills drafted by ministries are formally submitted by the deputies of the NC SR friendly to those ministries.

Another problem of law-making is the lack of systematic collection of data of application problems with respect to laws. Legislators draw up and politicians adopt the laws, however, regular employees of public administration bring them to life and observe the practical problems with their application. However, this valued experience from lower level of public administration is only seldomly exploited, for example through effective interpretation of these problems during the Interdepartmental Comments Procedure related to amendments of the law in question.

The governmental sessions debating bills pose another particular challenge. Whether a real exchange of views occur or there is only a formal adoption of the bill is based on multiple factors, such as whether there is a coalition or a one-party government, what the current political situation is, or how sensitive topic is discussed. It can be said that during the one-party rule of SMER-SD, there were situations when the debate in the government was only formal. Similarly, during the existence of coalition govern-

---

34 For example law firm GARANT PARTNER LEGAL, s.r.o. states at its webpage concrete examples of bills prepared for the official legislative process, available at https://www.gplegal.eu/clanok-0-36/54-Section-of-Legislation.html.

ments, the real discussion had often been shifted to the so-called coalition council composed of leaders of political parties forming the coalition.[35]

Significant factor in the drafting process is the relationship between politicians and the bureaucratic apparatus, whether in terms of political patronage or practical effectiveness of arguments of a professional in relation to a political solution. While examining the political patronage, it is important to draw attention to the fact that it concerns highly sensitive data and analyses based on "soft" data of daily press and statements of politicians in the media, rather than on real empirical analyses. An analysis attempting to determine the degree of political patronage in the Slovak Republic after 1989 claims that the highest degree of political patronage was during the Mečiar government between 1995 and 1998.[36] In 2002, the in power coalition government had introduced new system of civil services and established the Office for Civil Service with an aim to de-politicize nominations in civil service. However, the impact of the Office for Civil Service was limited and the body was subsequently even abolished.[37] In 2017, a new act on civil service was adopted with an aim to strengthen the independence and stability of civil service. Again a special independent coordinating and monitoring body for the protection of principles of civil service was established. However, given the short period of existence, it is too early to speak of the practical effectiveness of the new system of civil service.

The fate of governmental bills in the parliament

Although the key work on bills is almost always carried out at the executive level, there would be no laws without the parliament. It can be generally stated that the law-making activity in the Slovak Republic is intense

---

35 D Marek, 'Koaličná zmluva a jej ústavnoprávna (i)relevantnosť' (2017) Comenius Časopis. Available at https://comenius.flaw.uniba.sk/index.php/kategorie/politika-a-pravo/28-koalicna-zmluva-a-jej-ustavnopravna-i-relevantnost.

36 M Rybář, 'Powered by the State: The Role of Public Resources in Party-Building in Slovakia' (2006) 22 Journal of Communist Studies and Transition Politics 320-339.

37 Straňová and Malíková 2007, *ibid*, p. 299.

and increasingly hypertrophic.[38] If we focus for instance on the VI. electoral period (between years 2012 and 2016), 1372 bills were submitted to the NC SR. Out of these, 411 bills were submitted by the government and 957 bills by the deputies. 455 bills were approved, of which 382 (85 percent) were initiated by the government and only the rest by the deputies. Between 2016 and 2018, 221 out of 246 bills submitted by the government were adopted as laws.[39] Hence the success rate of governmental bills oscillated around very high 90 percent, making the government by far the most successful actor in proposing bills.

Although the executive level is a key legislative stage for preparing the content of bills, parliamentary level can also have a great impact on the content of bills. The discussions of bills in the NC SR goes through three readings. The first reading is primarily focused on the general discussion of the bill. The third reading consists mostly from voting on the bill. The second reading, taking place in the committees of the NC SR to which the bill has been assigned, as well as in the plenary, is the most significant in terms of the possibility to amend the content of the bill. While only one deputy suffices to submit amendments in the committees, at least 15 deputies are required to submit amendments and additions in the plenary. The second reading is also an opportunity for introduction of legislative improvements or elimination of any shortcomings by the ministry which submitted the bill. However, the ministers may not formally submit any changes and thus an "implicit" cooperation of a like-minded deputy who will formally introduce the amendment is required.

The bills or their amendments affect the public opinion or the opinion of interest groups on the minister or the political party represented by the minister. There is always a threat that interest groups or the public will mobilize the opposition and the media and the submission of unpopular bills is inevitably connected with a legislative tactic.[40] Therefore, in the second reading in the NC SR, it is possible to add things that the ministry

---

38 See L Cisko, 'Niekoľko úvah k tvorbe právnych predpisov v Slovenskej republike' in SK Bostan, RM Maksakova and TE Leonenko (eds), *Aktuaľni problemy deržavno-pravovoho rozvytku Ukrajiny v konteksti intehracijnych procesiv* (LIRA 2018) 17.

39 Functions of the National Council of the SR in the VI. electoral period – parliamentary study, p. 12-13.

40 See B Balog, 'Jazdci v legislatíve I - všeobecná charakteristika' (2001) 1 Notitiae ex Academia Bratislavensi Iurisprudentiae 4-13.

wanted to remain hidden. The bill on purpose does not contain unpopular elements at the executive stage of law-making, these are rather incorporated in the second reading. Obviously the willing deputy usually merely submits amendments drafted by the ministry. Legislative and technical amendments are often influenced by political purpose and tactical requirements determined by the effort of successfully passing the bill. Such a specific type of legislative tactic in the parliament is the specific division of the text of the proposed bill into parts (separate block of texts), so that other parts of the bill remain intact if there is a disagreement with one part. The division into multiple parts allows for separate voting on individual parts. It must be pointed out that governments and deputies affiliated with the government are not necessarily willing to take into account legislative requirements of the political parties of the opposition, unless a broader political consensus (constitutional majority) is required to adopt the bill.

Conclusion

The globalized world has an impact on the identity or similarity of the problems of the law-making. Among the most common mistakes in legal thinking (Slovakia included) is the assumption that everything that may be regulated must be regulated and the assumption that everything moral must be or become law.[41] In the context of lack of good legislators and other discussed problems of law-making in Slovakia,[42] the outcome leads to the instability of law, its lack of clarity and tension between the abstractness of law which reacts to the ever more complex world and *ad hoc* law-making caused by the attempt to prevent the circumvention of laws in cases when other social standards lose their effectiveness.[43] In one of his complaints against Timocrates, Demosthenes criticized the un-sound changes of legal order and described the example of the Greek town, Locris, which had ensured the elimination of ill-considered changes of le-

---

41 A Bröstl, 'Slova, slova, slova...' in A Gerloch and J Kysela, *Tvorba práva v České republice po vstupu do Evropské unie* (Wolters Kluwer 2007).

42 See H Magurová, 'Vybrané problémy tvorby práva v Slovenskej republike' in K Lenhartová and L Dufalová (eds), *Míľniky práva v stredoeurópskom priestore* (Univerzita Komenského v Bratislave 2012) 156-162.

43 M Večeřa, 'Diversita a jednota v právu' in *Zborník z medzinárodnej vedeckej konferencie Dny práva* (Masarykova univerzita 2008).

gal order and its stability in a truly original way. Whoever wanted to issue a new law in this city had to first put a loop around his/her neck and then present his/her bill before the assembly of the city's citizens. If the citizens of the city considered the bill as decent and just, the proposer left alive, if not, they pulled the loop around the neck of the proposer and strangled him.[44]

Ironically, it can be stated that there is no one to strangle recent legislators (and politicians as their initiators) and despite the almost perfect legal theories about legitimacy and legality of public power and the need for high-quality laws reflecting natural principles, there is a great erosion of quality of legislation. There has been a long-time consensus that laws do not fulfill the functions and objectives expected of them.[45] With less and less time reserved for drafting of a new regulation in practice, it is hard to create a legal act which will be internally consistent and will fit into the system created by a large number of existing legal regulations without any problems. Other shortcomings are generated by the multilingual legal order of the EU, mixing features of continental as well as common law. Linking such a complex legal order with national legal system is inevitably connected with legislative, technical and procedural problems.[46] These deficits in law-making undoubtedly leave a destructive trace in the trust of the public in the legal order and endanger the very foundations of democratic states based on the rule of law.

---

44 J Ober and Ch Hedrick, *Démokratia, a conversation on democracies, ancient and modern* (Princeton University Press 1996) 207.

45 P Kukliš, 'Právní normotvorba na Slovensku – vybrané problémy' in F Cvrček and F Novák (eds), *Legislativa: právní a teoretické problémy* (Aleš Čeněk 2017) 172.

46 See M Hodás, *Dopady normotvorby Európskej únie na normotvorbu členského štátu z hľadiska legislatívnej techniky a normotvorných procesov* (Univerzita Komenského v Bratislave 2018) 238.

Epilogue: Steppingstones for further research

Robert Zbíral

When citizens evaluate the quality of democracy (and political system as such), their opinions are closely tied to the ability of governments to make and implement policy.[1] The ministers know that their re-election is conditioned on the success of pursuing the benefits for citizens and thus strive to draft and subsequently assure adoption of bills that effectively contribute to that goal. As the chapter by Stefanou and Xanthaki describes, these objectives are common to all governments, yet they pursue quite distinguished strategies how to achieve them. The group of civil law countries, to which all states in our sample belong, shall share many similarities. However analyses in our volume reveal there are at the same time numerous particularities, reflected also in different perspectives the authors took, each of them emphasizing issues he found important for capturing "his" system. This situation makes a full-fledged comparative conclusion extremely difficult and it would be redundant to make mini summaries of each included case study. I will therefore further focus only on short comments on selected findings I considered generalisable and interesting, tentatively following research problems outlined in the introduction.

Constitutions of all included states obviously contain basic parameters of the legislative process, including roles of each involved state organ. Nonetheless the internal operations of the executive during drafting and negotiating bills are not constitutionally prescribed. Some states (Slovakia, Hungary, partly Poland) regulate at least selected aspects of those activities in special laws, others rely on specific governmental decree (the Czech Republic) or (non)binding set of manuals, circulars and guidelines (Austria, but they are widespread in other states as well). Executives draft the bills under watchful eyes of strong constitutional courts (namely Germany and the Czech Republic) that set certain rules and limits to the discretion of the governments, still the influence of the courts remains mostly

---

1 L Martin and G Vanberg, *Parliaments and Coalitions: The Role of Legislative Institutions in Multiparty Governance* (Oxford University Press 2011) 2.

pre-emptive as they have not yet annulled laws due to faults in the executive preparatory process.

Governmental bills are drafted by the administrators in relevant line
ministries, regularly with the assistance of legal departments, sometimes
the task is outsourced to external advisory companies or legal firms (e.g.
Slovakia, Austria, the Czech Republic). Subsequently consultations of the
bill are organised, this process is usually at least partly regulated by laws
or governmental decrees. Other ministries receive the chance to comment
on the bill in inter-ministerial consultations that might be either completely secret to external actors (Hungary) or transparently accessible on the
website (e.g. Poland, the Czech Republic). The right of consultation is regularly guaranteed to privileged subjects such as trade unions or employers
(Hungary, Poland, consocionalist tradition in Austria). In Slovakia or Austria even ordinary citizens may send their views on the bill. The impact of
consultations is dependent on numerous variables and will vary on case by
case basis, almost all authors however emphasize that if the government
wishes to limit negative comments, it simply changes the parameters of
the consultations (e.g. by shortening the traditional deadline for comments
or by narrowing the group of consultees) or circumvents the process altogether.

Regional units shall also operate as special consultees on the bills. Their
impact unsurprisingly correlates with the territorial organisation of the
states and is at its height in federations (Germany, Austria). In case of the
latter country the official institutions representing the interests of Länder
in the legislative arena are surprisingly side-lined, while the real power-
house is located in informal party ties between central and local politicians
(governors). None of the authors analysing other case studies mentioned
the involvement of regions in the preparation of bills, confirming the weak
position of self-government in post-communist states.

Legislative quality of bills shall be of the utmost significance for the
governments. This variable may be divided into two distinct elements: the
first relates to the legal quality of the bills' text itself (formal aspects like
comprehensibility or compliance with the rest of legal order), the second
relates to the effectiveness of their regulation (real impact). As to the former, while with the (now abandoned) exception of Poland no country from
our sample has used central independent body for drafting bills, the majority of states employs special subjects that review the formal quality of the
bill. Usually it is either a department at the Ministry of Justice (Germany)
or within the executive (Poland), the second option is subject consisting of

independent legal experts (Legislative Council in Slovakia or the Czech Republic). These bodies might have positive effects on the quality of bills but they only rarely interfere with the core content of the bill. As to the latter dimension of quality, evaluation of bills' effects has become obligatory and elaborate rules for performance of RIA were adopted in all states, but namely in the post-communist countries the process is often executed only formally and evaluation "helpfully" supports the solution preferred by the proposer.

The analysis of relationship between politicians and bureaucrats was only fleetingly discussed by majority of the authors. Yet the dilemma which of these two groups has higher influence during bills' preparation was clearly predominantly answered in favour of politicians. Civil servants are indispensable in providing expertise and drafting bills and could even succeed in pursuing their interests in case of less important bills, but once their views become incompatible with those of politicians, the will of ministers prevails. This outcome is probably predictable in post-communist countries that still have underdeveloped and politically dependent civil service, still the chapter on Austria plastically illustrates that even high-level entrenched bureaucrats with dozens of years of experience could not withstand pressure from newly appointed ministers with different political orientation.

Strategies of political parties within the (coalition) governments attracted more attention in the contributions. The anticipated models were confirmed: in traditional democracies (Austria, Germany), there is an effort to closely cooperate in preparation of most bills and "keep the tabs" on coalition partners. This approach is also facilitated by institutional rules, for example in Austria all bills must be adopted unanimously by the government before they are submitted to the parliament. In post-communist countries, ministers had much higher autonomy and the efficiency of constraining instruments was lower.[2] Coalition conflicts were common and strong and only limited energy was invested into wider coordination of legislative plans (the Czech Republic, Hungary); attempt to centralize the process by Prime Minister Tusk in Poland spectacularly failed. Yet this standard has been changing with the transformation of political scene. In Hungary the dominance of one party since 2011 has allowed to gain the Prime Minister

---

2 See also V Dimitrov et al, *Governing after Communism: Institutions and Policy-making* (Rowman & Littlefield 2006).

Orban complete control over the agenda of the government and subsequent proposition of bills and their adoption. In Poland, factionalism among ministers remains, but discretion over bills important for the leader of the ruling party J. Kaczynski is tightly constrained. Another issue that deserves notice in this respect is the widespread practice of submitting bills by the deputies of governmental parties directly in the parliament.[3] These "fake private bills" may serve either to speed up the process of adoption of certain bills (by skipping the steps within executive phase) or express hidden conflicts in the coalition and aim to circumvent coalition partners.

I believe that despite all distinction among cases and ensuing authors' approaches, the edited volume fulfilled its goal and illuminates many dark corners of the question "how the governments legislate". But the knowledge-gap on how the executives draft and negotiate bills and what impact their activities have on outputs of legislative process is far from fully bridged. Based on the knowledge we gained from descriptive analysis, scholars of legislative studies need to step up and formulate suitable theories and test them with real collected data. Because many of processes in the preparatory phase are internal to the government and officially unavailable to the public, such endeavour will be complicated. Yet that cannot stop our community from further exploration.

---

3 T Drinozcsi, 'Legislative Process' in U Karpen and H Xanthaki (eds), *Legislation in Europe: A Comprehensive Guide of Scholars and Practitioners* (Hart, 2017) 45.

Secondary sources cited in the book

Altman D, *Citizenship and Contemporary Direct Democracy* (Cambridge University Press 2018).

Andree A et al, 'Trust Is Good, Control Is Better: Multiparty Government and Legislative Organization' 69 (2016) Political Research Quarterly 108.

Aristotle, *Nichomachean Ethics* (D. Ross trans. 1980).

Badura P, *Staatsrecht: systematische Erläuterung des Grundgesetzes für die Bundesrepublik Deutschland* (C.H. Beck 2003).

Balog B and A Bonko, 'Legislatívne nič a ústavný súd' (2012) Notitiae ex Academia Bratislavensi Iurisprudentiae 4.

Balog B, 'Jazdci v legislatíve I - všeobecná charakteristika' (2001) Notitiae ex Academia Bratislavensi Iurisprudentiae 4.

Balog B, *Umenie tvoriť zákony, Schvaľovanie zákonov v Slovenskej republike* (Wolters Kluwer 2019).

Baraník K, 'Legislatívny proces v Slovenskej republike a jeho digitalizácia' in E Žatecká et al (eds), *Cofola: conference proceedings* (Masarykova univerzita 2011) 1572.

Bates SJ, 'United Kingdom' in U Karpen (ed), *Legislation in European Countries* (Nomos 1997) 431.

Beetham D, *Parliament and democracy in the twenty – first century, a guide to good practice* (Inter-parliamentary Union 2006).

Berek M, *Rada Ministrów jako organ inicjujący postępowanie ustawodawcze* (C.H. Beck 2017).

Bergeal B, *Rédiger un texte normatif* (Berger-Levrault 2012).

Biegelbauer P and PE Grießler, 'Politische Praktiken von Ministerialbeamt Innen im österreichischen Gesetzgebungsprozess' (2009) 38 Österreichische Zeitschrift für Politikwissenschaft 61.

Biegelbauer, P and S Mayer, 'Regulatory impact assessment in Austria: promising regulations, disappointing practices' (2008) 2 Critical Policy Analysis 123.

Birungi Kamugundu O, 'Prioritizing Legislation in the Policy Process' in H Xanthaki (ed), *Enhancing Legislative Drafting in the Commonwealth* (Routledge 2015) 85.

Blondel J, *Comparative Government: An Introduction* (Philip Allan 1990).

Bohadlo D et al (eds), *Legislativní proces (teorie a praxe)* (Ministerstvo vnitra 2011).

Bröstl A et al, *Ústavné právo Slovenskej republiky* (Aleš Čeněk 2010).

Bröstl A, 'Slova, slova, slova...' in A Gerloch and J Kysela, *Tvorba práva v České republice po vstupu do Evropské unie* (Wolters Kluwer 2007) 49.

Buckland W and AD McNair, *Roman Law and Common Law: A Comparison in Outline* (Cambridge University Press 1952).

Burch M, 'Organizing the Flow of Business in Western European Cabinets' in J Blondel and F Müller-Rommel (eds), *Governing Together* (Macmillan 1993) 99.

Burkhart S and M Lehnert, 'Between Consensus and Conflict: Law-Making Processes in Germany' (2008) 17 German Politics 223.

Bußjäger P, 'Föderalismus durch Macht im Schatten? Österreich und die Landeshauptmännerkonferenz' in *Jahrbuch des Föderalismus 2003. Föderalismus, Subsidiarität und Regionen in Europa* (Nomos 2003) 79.

Cibulka L et al, *Ústavné právo, Ústavný systém Slovenskej republiky* (Univerzita Komenského 2014).

Cisko L, 'Niekoľko úvah k tvorbe právnych predpisov v Slovenskej republike' in SK Bostan, RM Maksakova and TE Leonenko (eds), *Aktuaľni problemy deržavnopravovoho rozvytku Ukrajiny v konteksti intehracijnych procesiv* (LIRA 2018) 17

Clarence-Smith JA, 'Legislative drafting: English and Continental' (1980) 1 Statute Law Review 21.

Costain WD and AN Costain, 'Interest Groups as Policy Aggregators in the Legislative Process' (1981) 14 Polity 249.

Cox G and M McCubbins, *Setting the Agenda. Responsible Party Government in the U.S. House of Representatives* (Cambridge University Press 2005).

Crabbe V, 'Drafting in developing countries: the problems of importing expertise (1992) 4 African Journal of International and Comparative Law 645.

Crain M et al, 'Monopoly Aspects of Political Parties' (1979) 7 Atlantic Economic Journal 542.

Cvrček F et al., *Legislativa: Teoretická východiska a problémy* (Aleš Čeněk 2017).

David R, *Lustration and Transitional Justice. Personnel Systems in the Czech Republic, Hungary, and Poland* (University of Pennsylvania Press 2011).

Dickson B, *Introduction to French Law* (Pitman Publishing 1994).

Dimitrov V et al, *Governing after Communism: Institutions and Policymaking* (Rowman & Littlefield 2006).

Döring H, 'Time as a Scarce Resource: Government Control of the Agenda' in H Döring (ed) *Parliaments and Majority Rule in Western Europe* (Campus/St. Martin's Press 1995) 223.

Drgonec J, *Ústava Slovenskej republiky, Teória a prax* (C. H. Beck 2015).

Drinóczi T, *Minőségi jogalkotás és adminisztratív terhek csökkentése Európában* (HVG-ORAC 2010).

Drinóczi, T, 'Legislative Process' in U Karpen and H Xanthaki (eds), *Legislation in Europe: A Comprehensive Guide for Scholars and Practitioners* (Hart, 2017) 33.

Dunlop C and C Radaelli (eds), *Handbook of Regulatory Impact Assessment* (Edward Elgar 2016).

Dzieciuch M, 'Ocena polskiego procesu legislacyjnego na przykładzie ostatnich zmian w prawie rynków finansowych' (2018) 7 Internetowy Kwartalnik Antymonopolowy i Regulacyjny 8.

Editorial Review (1903) 22 Canadian Law Times 437.

Engle E, 'Aristotle, Law and Justice: The Tragic Hero' (2008) 35 Northern Kentucky Law Review 4.

Erk J, 'Austria: A Federation without Federalism' (2004) 34 Publius - The Journal of Federalism 1.

Escobar O, 'Pluralism and Democratic Participation: What Kind of Citizen are Citizens Invited to Be?' (2017) 14 Contemporary Pragmatism 416.

Evans C, *Addresses and Papers of Charles Evans Hughes, Governor of NY, 1906-1908* (Wentworth Press 2016).

Ewens J, 'Legislative Draftsmen: Their Recruitment and Training' (1983) 57 Australian Law Journal 567.

Fábry B, *Teoretické problémy tvorby práva* (A-Medi management 2018).

Fallend F, 'Austria: From Consensus to Competition and Participation?' in J Loughlin, F Hendriks and A Lidström (eds), *The Oxford Handbook of Local and Regional Democracy in Europe* (Oxford University Press 2010) 173.

Federal Ministry of Justice (ed), *Manual for Drafting Legislation* (Berlin 2008).

Filip J, 'K postavení Legislativní rady vlády České republiky' (2007) 15 Časopis pro právní vědu a praxi 203.

Filip J, *Vybrané kapitoly ke studiu ústavního práva* (Masarykova univerzita 2001).

Franczel R, 'Kormányzati döntéshozatal 2010-2014 között' (2015) Kodifikáció és Közigazgatás 5.

Gajduschek G, 'A közpolitikai célok megjelenése a jogban' in J Szerk and G Gajduschek (eds), *A magyar jogrendszer állapota* (MTA TK 2016) 43

Gajduschek G, 'Előkészítetlenség és utólagos hatásvizsgálat hiánya' in J Szerk and G Gajduschek (eds), *A magyar jogrendszer állapota* (MTA TK 2016) 796.

Giba M et al, *Ústavné pravo* (Wolters Kluwer 2019).

Goetz KH and R Zubek, 'Government, Parliament and Law-making in Poland' (2007) 13 The Journal of Legislative Studies 517.

Górniak J (ed), *Ocena wpływu oparta na dowodach. Model dla Polski* (Akademia Leona Koźmińskiego 2015).

Grodeland A and W Miller, *European Legal Cultures in Transition* (Cambridge University Press 2015).

Gyűrű A, 'A jogszabályok és a stratégiai tervek környezeti hatásvizsgálatának gyakorlata' (2012) Pro Futuro 85.

Haibo Y and Q Qianhong, 'Reservation of Law, Legislation and Human Rights Protection' 2 (2014) China Legal Science 92.

Hodás M, *Dopady normotvorby Európskej únie na normotvorbu členského štátu z hľadiska legislatívnej techniky a normotvorných procesov* (Univerzita Komenského v Bratislave 2018).

Hoyt MM, 'Education, Training and Retention of Legislative Draftsmen in Canada' (1979) 5 Commonwealth Law Bulletin 273.

Huber J and Ch Shipan, *Deliberate Discretion?: The Institutional Foundations of Bureaucratic Autonomy* (Cambridge University Press 2002).

Hull D, 'Commonwealth Survey of Terms and Conditions of Service of Legislative Draftsmen' (1984) 10 Commonwealth Law Bulletin 1359.

Ilonszki G and K Jager 'Hungary: Changing government advantages – Challenging a dominant executive' in E Rasch and G Tsebelis (eds), *Role of the governments in legislative agenda-setting* (Routledge 2011) 95.

Ilonszki G, 'From minimum to subordinate: A final Verdict? The Hungarian parliament, 1990–2010' (2011) 13 Journal of Legislative Studies 38.

Jugovits K, 'A jogalkotás tartalmi megalapozottsága a jogi oktatás tükrében' (2016) Pro Publico Bono – Magyar Közigazgatás 36.

Karlhofer F, 'A federation without federalism? Zur Realverfassung der Bund-Länder-Beziehungen' in P Bußjäger (ed), *Kooperativer Föderalismus in Österreich. Beiträge zur Verflechtung von Bund und Ländern* (Braumüller 2009) 131.

Karpen U and H Xanthaki (eds), *Legislation in Europe: A Comprehensive Guide for Scholars and Practitioners* (Hart, 2017).

Karpen U, 'Civil Service in Germany' (2019) 29 European Review of Public Law 1.

Karpen U, 'Comparative Law: Perspectives of Legislation' (2012) 6 Legisprudence 149.

Karpen U, 'Efficacy, Effectiveness, Efficiency' in K Meßerschmidt and AD Oliver-Lalana (eds), *Rational Lawmaking under Review, Legisprudence According to the German Federal Constitutional Court* (Springer 2016) 304.

Karpen U, 'Introduction' in U Karpen and H Xanthaki (eds), *Legislation in Europe: A Comprehensive Guide for Scholars and Practitioners* (Hart, 2017) 1.

Karpen U, 'Regulatory Impact Assessment (RIA): Current Situation and Prospects in the German Parliament' (2015) 101 Amicus Curiae 14.

Karpen U, I Breutz and A Nünke, Die Gesetzgebung der Großen Koalition in der ersten Hälfte der Legislaturperiode des 16. Deutschen Bundestages (2005-2007) (FHM Verlag 2008).

Khan-Freund O, C Lévy and B Rudden (eds), *A Source-book on French Law* (Clarendon Press 1990).

Kitschelt, H, Z Mansfeldova, R Markowski and G Toka, *Post-Communist Party Systems, Competition, Representation, and Inter-Party Cooperation* (Cambridge University Press 1999).

Kokeš M, 'Teorie zákonodárství aneb pokus čelit nezájmu právní teorie a politologie o legislativní tvorbu práva v ČR' (2016) 49 Správní právo (Legislativní příloha) I.

Kolář P, J Kysela, J Syllová, J Georgiev and J Pecháček, *Parlament České republiky* (Leges 2013).

Kopińska G, 'Rządowy proces legislacyjny' (2015) Analiza Programu Odpowiedzialne Panstwo 1.

Korn F, *Objektívne právo ako spoločenský normatívny system* (Tribun EU 2019).

Kukliš P, 'Právní normotvorba na Slovensku – vybrané problémy' in F Cvrček and F Novák (eds), *Legislativa: právní a teoretické problémy* (Aleš Čeněk 2017) 172.

Kysela J and M Kokeš, 'Role vlády v procesu právotvorby v České republice se zřetelem k efektivitě vládnutí' (2018) 51 Správní právo (Legislativní příloha) XC.

144

Kysela J, 'Moc výkonná jako činitel právotvorby. Přehled rolí a problémů' (2018) 51 Správní právo (Legislativní příloha) II.

Kysela J, 'The Influence of the Constitutional Court on the Rules of Legislative Process in the Czech Republic' (2014) Prague Law Working Papers Series II/4 1.

Kysela J, 'Tvorba práva v ČR: truchlohra se šťastným koncem?' (2006) 7 Právní zpravodaj 8.

Kysela J, *Dvoukomorové systémy: teorie, historie a srovnání dvoukomorových parlamentů* (Eurolex Bohemia 2004).

Ľalík T, 'Všeobecné a individuálne účinky derogačných nálezov Ústavného súdu SR' (2018) 70 Justičná revue 711.

Lando O, 'On legislative style and structure' (2006) 4 European Review of Private Law 476.

Laver M and KM Shepsle, *Making and Breaking Governments* (Cambridge University Press 1996).

Lehmbruch G, 'Sozialpartnerschaft in der vergleichenden Politikforschung' in P Gerlich, E Grande and WC Müller (eds), *Sozialpartnerschaft in der Krise* (Böhlau 2003) 129.

Liegl B and WC Müller, 'Senior Officials in Austria', in EC Page and V Wright (eds), *Bureaucratic Élites in Western European States* (Oxford University Press 1999) 100.

Lijphart A, *Patterns of Democracy: Government Forms and Performance in Thirty-six Countries* (Yale University Press 1999).

Lindblom C and D Cohen, *Usable Knowledge - Social Science and Social Problem Solving* (Yale University Press 1979).

Lortie S, 'Providing Technical Assistance on Law Drafting' (2010) 31 Statute Law Review 17.

Luther KR and WC Müller, 'Consociationalism and the Austrian political system' (1992) 15 West European Politics 1.

Maasen HG, 'Gesetzesinitiativen der Bundesregierung' in W Kluth and S Krings (eds), *Gesetzgebung: Rechtsetzung durch Parlamente und Verwaltungen sowie ihre gerichtliche Kontrolle* (C.F. Müller 2015) 191.

Magurová H, 'Vybrané problémy tvorby práva v Slovenskej republike' in K Lenhartová and L Dufalová (eds), *Míľniky práva v stredoeurópskom priestore* (Univerzita Komenského v Bratislave 2012) 156.

Mamojka M, 'Normotvorná a aplikačná stránka zákonnosti ako sinergia právneho štátu' in M Turošík and A Ševčiková (eds), *Banskobystrické dni práva na tému „Kvalita normotvornej a aplikačnej stránky zákonnosti ako determinant právneho štátu* (Belianum 2017) 5.

Markesinis B, H Unberath and A Johnston, *The German Law of Contract, A Comparative Treatise* (Hart Publishing 2006).

Markowska A and A Waszyńska, *Rządowy proces legislacyjny – opis procedur* (Rządowe Centrum Legislacji 2014).

Martin L and G Vanberg, *Parliaments and Coalitions: The Role of Legislative Institutions in Multiparty Governance* (Oxford University Press 2011).

Martin S et al (eds). *The Oxford Handbook of Legislative Studies* (Oxford University Press 2014).

Matyja R and B Sajduk, *Polska elita polityczna 2013* (WSE Kraków 2014).

McCubbins M and T Schwartz, 'Congressional Oversight Overlooked: Police Patrols versus Fire Alarms' (1984) 28 American Journal of Political Science 165.

Millet T, 'A comparison of French and British drafting (with particular reference to their respective nationality laws)' (1986) 7 Statute Law Review 153.

Müller WC and M Jenny 'Business as usual- mit getauschten Rollen oder Konflikt- statt Konsensdemokratie? Parlamentarische Beziehungen unter der ÖVP-FPÖ- Koalition' (2004) 33 Österreichische Zeitschrift für Politikwissenschaft 309.

Müller WC, 'Austria. Tight Coalitions and Stable Government' in WC Müller and K Strøm (eds), *Coalition Governments in Western Europe* (Oxford University Press 2000) 86.

Müller WC, 'Austria: A Complex Electoral System with Subtle Effects' in M Gallagher and P Mitchell (eds), *The Politics of Electoral Systems* (Oxford University Press 2008) 397.

Müller WC, 'Das Regierungssystem' in H Dachs et al (eds), *Politik in Österreich. Das Handbuch* (Manz 2006) 105.

Müller WC, 'Koalitionsabkommen in der österreichischen Politik' in G Becker, F Lachmayer and W Oberleitner (eds), *Gesetzgebung zwischen Politik und Bürokratie* (Österreichischer Bundesverlag 1994) 14.

Müller WC, 'Party Patronage and Party Colonization of the State' in W Crotty and RS Katz (eds), *Handbook of Party Politics* (Sage 2006) 175.

Müller WC, 'Party Patronage in Austria: Theoretical Considerations and Empirical Findings' in A Pelinka and F Plasser (eds), *The Austrian Party System* (Westview 1989) 327

Naurin E et al (eds), *Party Mandates and Democracy: Making, Breaking, and Keeping Election Pledges in Twelve Countries* (University of Michigan Press 2019).

Nikolenyi C and C Friedberg (2019) Vehicles of opposition influence or agents of the governing majority? Legislative committees and private members' bills in the Hungarian *Országgyűlés* and the Israeli *Knesset* (2019) 25 The Journal of Legislative Studies 358.

Norton P, *Parliaments in Western Europe* (Frank Cass 1990).

Nutting C, 'Legislative Drafting: A Review' (1955) 41 American Bar Association Journal 76.

Nzerem N, 'Prioritising Legislative Proposals in the Legislative Process' in A Zammit Borda (ed), *Legislative Drafting* (Routledge 2011) 57.

Ober J and Ch Hedrick, *Démokratia, a conversation on democracies, ancient and modern* (Princeton University Press 1996).

Obler R, 'Legislatures and the Survival of Political Systems: A Review Article' (1981) 96 Political Science Quarterly 127.

Ociepki T et al (eds), *Rząd pod lupą. Ranking polityk publicznych 2018* (Klub Jagiellonski 2019).

OECD, *OECD Regulatory Compliance Cost Assessment Guide* (Paris 2016).

Olson D and DM Norton, 'Legislatures in Democratic Transition' in D Olson and DM Norton (eds), *The New Parliaments of Central and Eastern Europe* (Frank Cass 1996) 1.

Olson D, *The legislative process: A comparative approach* (Harper and Row 1980).

Ost F. and M van de Kerchove, *Jalons pour une Theorie Critique du Droit* (Publications des Facultés universitaires Saint-Louis 1987).

Paczocha J, *Partia w Państwie: Bezprecedensowa wymiana kadr w administracji rządowej i jej legislacyjne podstawy* (FOR 2018).

Page E, *Policy Without Politicians: Bureaucratic Influence in Comparative Perspective* (Oxford University Press 2012).

Pelinka A, 'Gesetzgebung in politischen System Österreichs' in W Ismayr (ed), *Gesetzgebung in Westeuropa. EU-Staaten und Europäische Union* (VS-Verlag 2008) 446.

Pestalozza C, 'Gesetzgebung im Rechtsstaat' (1981) 39 Neue Juristische Wochenschrift 2084.

Pesti S and R Anikó-Franczel, 'A kormány működési és szervezeti rendje (1990–2014)' in A Körösényi (ed), *A magyar politikai rendszer – negyedszázad után* (Osiris 2015) 109.

Pesti S, 'Közpolitikai döntéshozatal Magyarországon' in G Gajduschek and T Rossiter (eds), *A közpolitika formálásának gyakorlata a brit és a magyar közigazgatásban* (Magyar Közigazgatási Intézet 2002) 153.

Pigeon LP, *Drafting and Interpreting Legislation* (Carlswell 1988).

Pigeon LP, *Rédaction et interprétation des lois* (Gouvernement du Québec 1986).

Piris JC, 'The legal orders of the European Union and of the Member States: peculiarities and influences in drafting' (2006) 8 European Journal of Law Reform 1.

Plichtová J, 'Občianska deliberatívna demokracia a podpora jej cieľov na Slovensku' (2010) 42 Sociológia 516.

Power T, 'Time and Legislative Development in New Democracies: Is Executive Dominance Always Irreversible?' in R Pelizzo et al (eds), *Trends in Parliamentary Oversight* (World Bank Institute 2004) 47.

Rasch BE and G Tsebelis (eds), *The Role of Governments in Legislative Agenda Setting* (Routledge, 2011).

Roman C et al, *Analýza, monitor merania administratívneho a regulačného zaťaženia podnikania* (Centrum vzdelávania MPSVR SR 2014).

Rybář M, 'Powered by the State: The Role of Public Resources in Party-Building in Slovakia' (2006) 22 Journal of Communist Studies and Transition Politics 320.

Saiegh SM, 'Lawmaking' in S Martin, T Saalfeld and KW Ström (eds), *The Oxford Handbook of Legislative Studies* (OUP 2014) 481.

Saiegh SM, 'Political Prowess or "Lady Luck"? Evaluating Chief Executives' Legislative Success Rates' (2009) 71 The Journal of Politics 1342.

Salgó LP, *Az Igazságügyi Minisztérium szerepe a kormányzati jogszabály-előkészítésben* (Fontes Iuris 2017).

Sartori G, 'Compare Why and How. Comparing, Miscomparing and the Comparative Method.' in M Dogan and A Kazancigil (eds), *Comparing Nations: Concepts, Strategies, Substance* (Blackwell 1994) 16.

Schaden M, 'Verfassungsgerichtsbarkeit' in H. Dachs et al. (eds), *Politik in Österreich. Das Handbuch* (Manz 2006) 213.

Scharffs BG, 'Law as Craft' (2001) 45 Vanderbilt Law Review 2339.

Schefbeck G, 'Das Parlament' in H Dachs et al (eds), *Politik in Österreich* (Manz Verlag 2006) 152.

Schneider H, *Gesetzgebung: ein Lehr- und Handbuch* (C.F. Müller 2002).

Schultze RO, 'Föderalismus' in D Nohlen (ed), *Lexikon der Politik, Vol. 3: Die westlichen Länder* (1992 Beck Verlag) 108.

Schwarz J and E Shaw, *The United States Congress in Comparative Perspective* (Dryden Press 1976).

Seidman AW, RB Seidman and N Abeyeskere, *Legislative Drafting for Democratic Social Change: Manual for Drafters* (Kluwer Law 2001).

Shepshle K, 'Rational Choice Institutionalism' in S Binder et al (eds), *The Oxford Handbook of Political Institutions* (Oxford University Press 2008).

Sickinger H, 'Parlamentarismus' in E Talos (ed), *Schwarz-Blau. Eine Bilanz des Neu-Regierens* (LIT Verlag 2006) 76.

Škop M and B Vacková, 'Být legislativcem: Empirická šetření v administrativních fázích legislativy' (2019) 27 Časopis pro právní vědu a praxi 5.

Smuk P, 'Az Országgyűlés' in J Szerk and G Gajduschek, *A magyar jogrendszer állapota* (MTA TK 2016) 631.

Somolányi S, 'Slovakia: From a Difficult Case of Transition to a Consolidated Central European Democracy' in T Hayashi (ed), *Democracy and Market Economics in Central and Eastern Europe: Are New Institutions Being Consolidated?* (SRC 2004) 149.

Šramel B, *Ústavné súdnictvo* (Občianske združenie FSV 2015).

Stark J, 'Should the Main Goal of Statutory Drafting Be Accuracy or Clarity?' (1994) 15 Statute Law Review 207.

Stark, J 'The Proper Degree of Generality for Statutes' (2004) 25 Statute Law Review 77.

Staroňová K and L Malíková, 'The view of political science on the phenomenon of corruption' (2007) 39 Sociológia 287.

Staroňová K, 'Regulatory Impact Assessment: Formal Institutionalization and Practice' (2010) 30 Journal of Public Policy 1202.

Stefanou C, *'Comparative Legislative Drafting: Comparing Across Legal Systems'* (2016) 18 European Journal of Law Reform 123.

Stefanou C, 'Drafters, Drafting and the Policy Process' in C Stefanou and H Xanthaki (eds) *Drafting legislation: a modern approach* (Ashgate 2008) 321.

Strom K et al. (eds), *Cabinets and Coalition Bargaining: The Democratic Life Cycle in Western Europe* (Oxford University Press 2008).

Svák J and B Balog, 'Legislatívna kultúra' (2018) 101 Právny obzor 345.

Svák J et a., *Teória a prax legislatívy* (Eurokódex 2012).

Svák J, Ž Surmajová and B Balog, *Zákon o tvorbe právnych predpisov a o Zbierke zákonov Slovenskej republiky: Komentár* (Wolters Kluwer 2017).

Szabó Z, 'Hozzáadott érték benyújtás és elfogadás között: viták és módosító javaslatok az Országgyűlésben 2006–2016 között' (2017) Parlamenti Szemle 25.

Tálos E and B Kittel, *Gesetzgebung in Österreich. Netzwerke, Akteure und Interaktionen in politischen Entscheidungsprozessen* (WUW 2001).

Tálos E, 'Sozialpartnerschaft. Austrokorporatismus am Ende?' in H Dachs et al. (eds), *Politik in Österreich. Das Handbuch* (Manz 2006) 425.

Tetley W, *Marine Cargo Claims* (Les Éditions Yvon Blais 1988).

Treib O, 'Party Patronage in Austria: From Reward to Control in P. Kopecky, P Mair and M Spirova (eds), *Party Patronage and Party Government in European Democracies* (Oxford University Press 2012) 31.

Tsebelis G, *Veto Players. How Political Institutions Work* (Princeton University Press 2002).

Večeřa M, 'Diversita a jednota v právu' in *Zborník z medzinárodnej vedeckej konferencie Dny práva* (Masarykova univerzita 2008).

Vedral J, 'K příčinám nynějšího stavu právního řádu a k možnostem vlády při jeho (re)formování' in A Gerloch and J Kysela (eds), *Tvorba práva v České republice po vstupu do Evropské unie* (ASPI 2007) 87.

Voermans W et al (eds), *Legislative Process in Transition* (Leiden University Press 2012).

Voermars W, 'Legislation and Regulation' in U Karpen and H Xanthaki (eds), *Legislation in Europe: A Comprehensive Guide for Scholars and Practitioners* (Hart 2017)

von Kirchmann SU, *Die Werlosigkeit der Jursprudenz als Wissenschaft* (Verlage von Julius Springer 1848).

Voermans W, 'Styles of Legislation and Their Effects' (2011) 32 Statute Law Review 38.

Watts L, *Comparing Federal Systems* (McGill Queen's University Press 1999).

Wilfling P, *Zákon o slobodnom prístupe k informáciám, komentár, problémy z praxe, rozhodnutia súdov* (Via Iuris 2015).

Wineroither D, *Kanzlermacht-Machtkanzler?: Die Regierung Schüssel im historischen und internationalen Vergleich* (LIT Verlag 2009).

Wintr J, *Česká parlamentní kultura* (Auditorium 2010).

Wołek A, *Rząd do remontu, Raport Centrum Analiz Klubu Jagiellońskiego* (Klub Jagiellonski 2015).

Xanthaki H, 'EU Legislative quality post-Lisbon: the challenges of Smart Regulation' (2014) 35 Statute Law Review 66.

Xanthaki H, 'On transferability of legislative solutions: the functionality test' in C Stefanou and H Xanthaki (eds), *Drafting Legislation: A Modern Approach – in Memoriam of Sir William Dale* (Aldershot 2008) 1.

Xanthaki H, *Drafting Legislation: Art and Technology of Rules for Regulation* (Hart 2014).

Zander M, *The Law-Making Process* (Hart 2015).

Zbíral R, 'Legislative process in the Czech Republic' in H Xanthaki and U Karpen (eds) *Legislation in European Countries* (Hart, in print).

Zubek R, 'Negative Agenda Control and Executive–Legislative Relations in East Central Europe, 1997–2008' (2011) 17 The Journal of Legislative Studies 172.

Zubek R, H Klüver, 'Legislative pledges and coalition government' 21 (2015) Party Politics 603.

Žuffová M, *Slovenská republika: špeciálna hodnotiaca správa 2014 – 2015* (Iniciativa pro otvorené vládnutí 2016).

Zweigert K and H Kötz, *An Introduction to Comparative Law* (Oxford University Press 1998).

List of contributors

Milan Hodás, Associate Professor of Constitutional Law, Comenius University, Faculty of Law in Bratislava, Researcher at the Institute of state and law of the Slovak Academy of Science. For more than six years, he directly participated in legal approximation and oversight over the approximation process as the Legal Advisor at the Department of Legislation and Law Approximation of the Chancellery of the National Council of the Slovak Republic. Later, he worked also for the Ministry of Education, Science, Research and Sport, European Affairs Committee of the Slovak Parliament, where he dealt with judicial cooperation in civil and criminal matters, as well as with the Schengen area. He worked for two years as Director of the Parliamentary Institute of the Chancellery of the National Council of the Slovak Republic. He has authored two books and dozens of articles. Email: milan.hodas@gmail.com

Ulrich.Karpen, Professor of Constitutional and Administrative Law, University of Hamburg; member of the Hamburg state parliament (1991–2001); former chairman of the International Association of Legislation and of the German Association of Legislation, member of the editorial board of "Zeitschrift für Gesetzgebung (ZG)"; author of *Legistics—Freshly Evaluated,* 2nd enlarged edn (Baden-Baden, Nomos, 2008); and 'Comparative Law: Perspectives of Legislation' [2012] Legisprudence 149; Email: ulrich.karpen@gmx.de

Marian Kokeš, Senior Lecturer at the Faculty of Law of the Palacky University Olomouc, Department of Constituional Law, where he teaches constitutional law, human rights law and political party law. He is also a judge of the Regional Administrative Court in Brno. Email: marian.kokes@upol.cz.

Eric Miklin, Associate Professor of Political Science at the University of Salzburg, specializing in Comparative Politics, especially political parties and legislative institutions. His research has been published in journals such as West European Politics, the Journal of European Public Policy and the Journal of Common Market Studies. Email: eric.miklin@sbg.ac.at

Jacek Sokolowski, Director, Centre for Quantitative Research in Political Science Jagiellonian University. Graduated in Law at the Jagiellonian University in 2000, in 2005 obtained his doctorate degree from Heidelberg University and has been working both as a lawyer and as an academic ever since. Interests: law-making processes from an empirical perspective, behavioural patterns of parliamentary groups the judiciary as an element of the political system. The author of, among other things, *Wybrane aspekty funkcjonowanie Sejmu w latach 1997-2007* and a co-creator of ISQAL database system for the quantitative analysis of parliamentary activity. Email: jacek.sokolowski@uj.edu.pl

Constantin Stefanou, Director, Sir William Dale Centre for Legislative Studies, IALS, University of London. Author of *Legislative Drafting and the Policy Process,*2008; Drafters , Drafting and the Policy Process, in: C Stefanou and H .Xanthaki (eds), *Drafting Legislation:A modern Approach.* Ashgate, pp 321-333; Comparative Legislative Drafting, (2016),European Journal of Law Reform, 2/2016, pp.123-138. Email: constantin.stefanou@sas.ac.uk

Zsolt Szabó, associate professor of constitutional law at Károli Gáspár University of the Reformed Church in Hungary, and senior research fellow at National University of Public Service. His main research interests are comparative constitutional law, legislation, legislative drafting and parliamentary procedures. Email: Szabo.Zsolt@uni-nke.hu

Helen Xanthaki, Faculty of Laws, University College London; Dean, Postgraduate Law programmes, University of London; President, International Association for Legislation; author of *Drafting Legislation: Art and Technology of Rules for Regulation* (oxford, Hart publishing, 2014); and *Thornton's Legislative Drafting,* 5th edn (London, Bloomsbury, 2013); member of the editorial board of *Theory and Practice of Legislation.* Email: h.xanthaki@ucl.ac.uk

Robert Zbíral, Associate Professor at the Masaryk University in Brno and Palacky University in Olomouc. He teaches mainly constitutional and European law. His research focuses on division of competences between the EU and its Member States, implementation of EU law and legislative process at the national level. He has authored five books and dozens of articles (i.e. in Common Market Law Review, Journal of European Public

Policy) and book chapters (i.e. in Oxford University Press, Hart Publishing). Apart from pursuing academic career, he also works part-time as assistant to a judge of the Czech Constitutional Court and as a member of the Working Group for EU law at the Czech Government Office. Email: robert.zbiral@law.muni.cz

Summary

In almost all states, laws (statutes) serve as the most important instruments to prompt social, economic or institutional change. Parliaments traditionally used to be considered as the locus of law-making, yet observers of politics pointed out that it had rather been the government (executive) that affects the outputs of the legislative game more prominently. Statistical data reveal that in most cases the governmental bills submitted to parliaments are adopted unchanged. Despite that little attention has been aimed at the previous phase of the legislative process: drafting and negotiating of bills within the executives. This book narrows the knowledge gap and analyse in detail who and how prepare the bills in their "cradle". Six countries of Central Europe were selected for the analysis to provide comparable knowledge. The chapters, written by experienced scholars with local knowledge, have both descriptive and analytical dimensions and evaluate also practical functioning of the system in each state.